Meditation Is Boring?

Meditation Is Boring?

Putting Life in Your Spiritual Practice

Linda Johnsen

The Himalayan Institute Press
Honesdale, Pennsylvania

The Himalayan Institute Press
RR 1 Box 405
Honesdale, PA 18431

8   7   6   5   4   3   2   1

Cover design by Michele Wetherbee
Page design by Joan Gazdik Gillner

This book is printed on acid-free paper. ∞

Library of Congress Cataloging-in-Publication Data

Johnsen, Linda, 1954–
    Meditation is boring? : putting life in your spiritual practice /
Linda Johnsen.
        p. cm.
    ISBN 0–89389–179–7 (pb : alk. paper)
    1. Spiritual life—Hinduism. I. Title.

BL1237.36 .J64 2000
294.5'435—dc21   99-088453

For the guru parampara

Contents

Acknowledgments

I'D LIKE TO GRATEFULLY acknowledge Deborah Willoughby and the rest of her staff at *Yoga International* for their efforts in bringing authentic information about the yoga tradition to the public. I don't think most students realize how much hard work producing a magazine like this entails, but as a regular contributor, I've watched the staff in action over the years, and I'm still awed! This book grew out of an article I wrote for *YI* some years ago, complaining about how tedious spiritual practice can be.

Many thanks to Anne Craig for nursing this manuscript through the editing process. Special thanks to Pandit Rajmani Tigunait, who encouraged me to write the book in the first place!

Love and kisses to Johnathan Brown, my partner on the path. I'd also like to acknowledge my many friends from the Himalayan Institute, the Devi Mandir, and the M.A. Center who share the adventure. A special note to Janine Canan, Gayatri (Patricia Marx), Beverly Miller, and Cynthia Bretheim: thanks for keeping me company!

With soul-felt appreciation I bow to my spiritual teachers. Like lamps in the night, they light the way.

And with loving reverence I bow to Mother Sarasvati, from whom this whole matrix of maya and moksha emerged in the first place. To the Mother of the Universe, I bow again and again!

chapter one

At the Heels of the Master

IN 1970 Swami Rama overturned the world. Under the watchful eyes of scientists at the Menninger Foundation in Topeka, Kansas, Swamiji demonstrated that he could raise and lower the temperature of particular cells in his body at will and bring his heart to a virtual, fluttering stop. To demonstrate the physical effects of advanced yoga practices, he mimicked brain death—at first lab technicians thought their EEG had broken down, but no sooner had they verified that the equipment was in perfect working order than the electrodes attached to Swamiji's skull once again registered a flat line. He was in *samadhi*, a particularly deep state of meditation, he explained.

Swamiji played with the research team for several weeks. In an attempt to teach them that "all of the brain is in the mind but not all of the mind is in the brain," Swamiji put himself into a state of deep sleep—which characteristically shows up on the EEG in the form of steady delta waves. When the researchers woke the snoring swami sometime later he accurately reported every conversation that had been going on nearby while he was "asleep." The scientists were staggered. How was this possible?

At another point Swami Rama boasted that the yogis of the Himalayas could move objects without touching them. Then, during a lab experiment painstakingly designed to prevent any possibility of fraud, he focused his attention on a needle mounted at its center to a small metal spindle. Suddenly, before the disbelieving eyes of researchers, the end of the needle lurched through an arc of nearly sixty degrees. While the Menninger staff dutifully reported most of the results of their research to the scientific community, making Swami Rama an overnight celebrity, they refrained from publishing the final results for years, fearing they would lose their scientific credibility if they admitted seeing what they actually saw.

You would think that with powers and abilities like these, copiously documented under the most stringent laboratory conditions and widely reported in the press, Swami Rama would look up to see hundreds of scientists beating a path to his door. But in fact, during the two decades he spent visiting the West, most scientists avoided him like the plague. If he had something extraordinary to teach, they didn't want to know. Swami Rama was challenging the most basic assumptions of Western science regarding mind and matter, demonstrating that the physiology textbooks needed to be rewritten, and shaking the very foundations of physics—and they wanted no part of it. Swami Rama's guru, Bengali Baba, had sent him to America to reveal to Western scientists the unlimited vistas of human consciousness, but they wouldn't come near him with a ten-foot pole. They didn't like having their most fundamental concepts about reality called into question.

Meeting the Master

I met Swamiji fairly early in the game, in 1971, when he was still full of confidence that the Western academic community would ultimately come around. Fifty-ish, he was a huge man, well over six feet tall, lively and robust, who spoke surprisingly good English. He wore a long white robe with one end thrown over his shoulder (which made him look somewhat like an ancient Roman senator), rather than the traditional ocher robe of India's orthodox swami lineages. But there was nothing orthodox about him—Swamiji played by his own rules. He loved nothing better than deliberately upsetting everyone's expectations and mercilessly confusing the well-meaning yoga students who showed up hoping to witness the psychic phenomena he was reputed to perform. Some debated whether he was enlightened or just plain crazy—I personally suspected, though I couldn't always prove, that there was method in his madness.

I moved two blocks from Swami Rama's ashram in Glenview, Illinois, in the fall of 1976 to enroll in the master's-degree Program in Eastern Studies he was setting up just north of Chicago. I figured that Swamiji was lucky to have me, a straight-A student from a prestigious college, already widely read in Eastern philosophy (something rare in those days). But when I'd answer a question in his class on the *Yoga Sutra* he'd shout that I was wrong, whether I was wrong or not. I'd turn in well-written papers for his *Upanishads* course which would come back marked "D" or "F." As I'd pore over page after page through which he'd drawn thick red "X's," trying to figure out what could possibly be the matter with what I'd said, I finally realized that he hadn't actually read the paper— he'd gone through it crossing out paragraphs arbitrarily. It wasn't my work he didn't like, it was my attitude.

I always had the uncomfortable feeling that Swamiji saw through me like a window. One evening I seriously considered cutting his class; one of my favorite Shakespearean dramas, *Henry IV, Part 2*, was on television that night. As an ex-English major, I reviewed scenes from the play in my mind all the way to class, thinking, "The complete works of Shakespeare is the greatest book in the English language."

As he launched into his lecture that night, Swamiji interrupted himself, apropos of nothing. "Shakespeare is not the greatest book in the English language!" he shouted. "Bible is the greatest book in English!" I was startled, but reassured myself that his remark was a coincidence. Then he turned around, looked me in the eye, and barked, "Isn't that right, student of English?" I nearly fell out of my chair.

One morning Swami Rama walked into the room where I sat working, the princess of Nepal and her husband in tow. Swamiji's eyes started to twinkle and I knew I was in trouble. "This is Linda," he told his guests. "She's a witch!"

A friend of mine standing nearby broke in, "Oh no, Swamiji, Linda is a wonderful person." But I was dumbstruck. Before heading in to work that morning I'd been reading a classic feminist book on the valued role of women in pagan religions. "If I weren't already committed to yoga, I'd be a witch," I'd thought to myself.

Swami Rama played hardball with his students, and it's no wonder some of them left in disgust. One morning as I was out jogging I was so angry at him I was practically frothing at the mouth. "No one has the right to treat people the way he does," I thought furiously. "Enlightened master or not, he should be subject to the rules of human decency like the rest of us!" Although I have many vices, violence is not usually one of them; but this morning I was so infuriated I actually visualized slamming Swamiji over the head with a baseball bat.

Later that day Swamiji stopped by after a tennis game. Without uttering a word he walked over to me, slammed me over the head with his tennis racquet, winked, and walked away.

It was hard to know what to make of the guy personally, but there's no question that as a teacher of the yoga tradition he was unexcelled. Swamiji made sure we knew the *Yoga Sutra* backwards and forwards, that we understood at least the basic principles of the six major schools of Indian philosophy, and that we had some grasp of the amazing history of the yoga tradition. He wanted us to understand how the physical body works so we could see why hatha yoga is so valuable. He wanted us to understand how the subtle body works so we could see why the breathing exercises yogis call pranayama are so important. He wanted us to understand how the mind works so we could understand how to meditate properly. He wanted us to know what the higher self is so we could actually experience it in meditation.

The numerous teachers Swamiji had assembled for his fledgling college were superb: top scholars from India who lived what they taught and thereby made the teaching come alive for us, top scholars from America steeped in both Eastern and Western mysticism, and a bevy of physicians and psychologists capable of translating the sophisticated *vidyas* (inner sciences) of yoga into terms Americans could understand. Barbara Brown, leader of the biofeedback revolution, showed us how yoga training can be accelerated with the sophisticated equipment students have access to today. Rudolph Ballentine, M.D., one of the original movers and shakers in the whole-foods movement, taught us yogic physiology and Ayurvedic principles of nutrition.

Swamiji also pulled strings to get us the best visiting "professors" from various traditions: Sri Chitrabhanu, the inspired Jain monk; Rabbi Gelberman, the Kabbalist;

Lama Jamspal, who taught us *The Tibetan Book of the Dead;* Pir Vilayat Khan, who introduced us to Sufi mysticism; Swami Satchidananda and Swami Bua, who, like Swamiji himself, lived the yoga tradition. Later New Age conferences would pull luminaries like these together routinely, but Swami Rama was one of the first educators since the World Parliament of Religions in 1893 to throw out distinctions between different religions and ask us to see the truth in all of them.

The graduate program burst its britches: there wasn't enough room for all the students; some classes met outside under the trees. Students appeared from everywhere: hard-core researchers from major universities may have been giving Swami Rama wide berth, but the public was anxious to learn more. Swamiji appeared on *The Phil Donahue Show,* in *People* magazine, and earned himself an impressive mention in the *Encyclopaedia Britannica.* At the same time, Maharishi Mahesh Yogi was sponsoring research into the benefits of meditation and managed to get the results published in scientific journals, Swami Satchidananda presided at Woodstock, Swami Muktananda brought *shaktipata* initiation to the masses, and Prabhupad Bhaktivedanta persuaded American youth to shave their heads and dance in the streets chanting *"Hare Krishna."* Yoga was happening. Drugs were out, basmati rice was in.

Swamiji moved his graduate school to northeastern Pennsylvania, where land was cheap, purchasing an abandoned Catholic seminary for a song. While accreditation was being arranged I kept the home fires burning, managing the Center for Holistic Medicine Swamiji founded in Glenview. Our physicians recommended unheard-of new treatment modalities such as regular physical exercise, vegetarian diets based on whole foods, meditation, homeopathic remedies, and stress-reduction techniques like yoga and breathing exercises. The radical nature of our medical practice precipitated an American Medical Association investigation as medical lawyers, outraged at our unorthodox methodology, tried to shut us down. But when investigators from the A.M.A. saw what kinds of results we were getting, they recommended that the lawsuit be dropped—and one of them snuck back to my desk and asked me to schedule an appointment for him. People forget what a major player Swami Rama was in getting the holistic health movement rolling in the early 1980s.

After my first husband and I split, my relationship with Swamiji improved substantially. I was trying to talk with Swamiji about something suitably academic when the anguish of the failed marriage spilled out of my eyes and I started bawling like a child. Well, the Himalayan taskmaster turned out to have a heart after all. He enveloped me in one of his justly famous bear hugs, compassion oozing from every pore in his body. He landed me a fantastic new job and arranged for a full scholarship through graduate school. He also kept me near him for a summer or two—an amazing experience which allowed me to watch the master up close. Often people dismiss Swamiji's extraordinary accomplishments—arriving in the U.S. friendless and penniless, yet almost immediately helping precipitate the wave of passion for yoga which flooded America and Europe in the '70s. But who would expect less from a Himalayan master? Working so closely with Swamiji, however, it became apparent that he was still working on himself like the rest of us, though at a level beyond what most of us could probably comprehend—a hard-working human being whose incredible achievements resulted from years of struggle and self-sacrifice, who was in some ways still as brazen and fallible as he candidly portrayed himself in his classic autobiography,

Living with the Himalayan Masters. Getting to know Swamiji personally took the edge off my awe, but made me appreciate the magnitude of his attainments all the more.

Swamiji eventually retired back to India, where he devoted his still considerable energies to founding a hospital city near Rishikesh for mountain people who had no access to medical services (not just a hospital, a "hospital city"—Swamiji always thought big). When Swamiji left his body in November 1996 some people were relieved that the uncontrollable yogi with the outrageous manners was finally gone. But thousands of holy men streamed out of the Himalayas for his funeral, honoring one of the greatest of their own.

Some of the information Swamiji and the other yogis who came to America in the 1970s brought with them did manage to leak through into popular Western culture. Stress-management techniques culled directly from yoga are taught at most major medical facilities these days, hatha classes are ubiquitous, the value of a meatless diet is widely recognized, the concept of reincarnation is no longer utterly foreign, and most people have a hazy idea that if they meditated, it would probably do them some good. But the inner essence of yoga has still not percolated through to the average American. That there really is an immortal inner self, that if we calm our mind the guidance and inspiration of this higher being can shine through into our daily lives, that we can all literally experience extraordinary mystical states, are realities beyond the ken of most Westerners.

Since Swami Vivekananda first brought yoga to Western shores in 1893, great Indian masters like Sri Yukteswar, Neem Karoli Baba, Nityananda, and Bengali Baba repeatedly expressed their concern for Western students by sending over spiritual mentors to introduce us to our innermost self.

As we enter the twenty-first century the latest wave of teachers from the East is renewing the assault on our limited Western concept of our spiritual potential. As a roving journalist covering the yoga beat, I've been fortunate to meet quite a few of them. Importantly, many of the new teachers are women: Ammachi, Shree Maa, Karunamayi, Anandi Ma, Gurumayi, Ma Yoga Shakti. They are bringing a bracing new dimension to the teaching of yoga in the West, reasserting the value of love and devotion, in addition to technical mastery of yogic technique. Just as a little yeast raises a lot of dough, the timeless tradition of yoga continues to uplift the consciousness of Western culture. I for one am profoundly grateful to the *parampara*, the lineage of gurus, whose ceaseless grace knows no national boundary.

Is a Guru Really Necessary?

In the 1980s a backlash against the role of the guru began gathering momentum in the West. Occasional devotees have gone so far as to suggest that the guru system needs to be jettisoned altogether—we're fully capable of achieving enlightenment without a guru from India or anywhere else. This is rather like announcing that we're going to found a colony on Mars but we're not going to use any of the data collected by the American or Russian space programs to help us.

Part of the reason for the backlash is that realized masters are seldom committed to living up to our image of how they should behave. We want them to be wholly divine—discovering that they're also human can be a disillusioning shock for overly zealous devotees. Swami Rama often laughed about the Indian woman who fainted when she learned that he actually had to use the toilet.

The other, more serious, part of the problem is that

quite a few guru figures have been embroiled in scandals: Hindu, Buddhist, Christian, Jewish—one religious leader after another has danced in the unflattering spotlight of press exposés. Unfortunately scandals have always been with us. Several of the early Christian manuscripts discovered near Nag Hammadi in 1945 describe the discomfort of Jesus' disciples over his intimacy with Mary Magdalene, and early Buddhist histories report that the Buddha himself actually stood trial for allegedly assaulting a nun (he was acquitted). Whether the claims are true or not, they can profoundly undermine our confidence in our spiritual mentors and their teachings. Do rumors like these mean we should no longer respect Buddha or Jesus and must abandon their teachings? Or do they mean that all of us, teacher and student alike, must get clearer on the emotionally charged issues surrounding sexuality?

One of my professors, a brilliant young pandit from the Banaras area, had enormous faith in Swami Rama. But Swamiji knew how to shake everyone up, and Pandit Tigunait was no exception. Swamiji had promised to reveal the mantras of his lineage to a follower named Brunette so that she could begin initiating students in his meditation tradition. However, whenever she'd appear at the appointed time Swamiji would claim he was busy and ask her to come back in another few days. This went on for several weeks, but Brunette had been around the block with Swamiji and understood that he was testing her level of sincerity and motivation. Finally one day Swamiji announced that since he was too busy to meet with her himself, Pandit Tigunait would teach her the mantras. Panditji was shocked when he heard the news; he had no clue to what they were. Now it was Panditji knocking on Swamiji's door, asking to learn the mantras of the lineage but repeatedly being turned away.

For the first time, Panditji began to doubt Swami Rama. Maybe Swamiji didn't actually know the mantras and wanted Panditji to make some up. As the hour approached when he'd promised to meet with Brunette, Panditji sat down and, his heart breaking, fabricated a list of mantras out of thin air. Some he'd heard from other yoga masters, others he'd read in various sacred texts.

Brunette was ecstatic to receive the transmission, but Panditji was so upset at having participated in such a fraud that he burst into Swamiji's room, threw the list down at Swamiji's feet, and cried, "There are the mantras I gave your disciple—I hope you're satisfied!"

Swamiji turned to his secretary and commanded, "Bring me the manuscript my guru's guru gave me." She brought in a traditional Tibetan book: oblong parchment sheets filled with Sanskrit and Tibetan verses, pressed between two boards and wrapped in cloth. Panditji opened the book at random, and there on the page in front of him were exactly the same mantras he'd given Brunette, in exactly the same order he'd given them to her.

Panditji was so overwhelmed that he started to cry. He turned to Swami Rama to ask for forgiveness, but Swamiji's face was black with rage. "How dare you think it was you giving the mantras!" he shouted.

So who gave the mantras? The point I'm trying to make is that the guru gave the mantras—but we need to understand what the guru actually is. According to the *Bhavana Upanishad*, "*Shakti* is the guru." That is, divine energy, supreme consciousness itself, is the guru. It uses the human person we call the guru as a vehicle, the way electricity transmits itself through copper wire. The parampara, the lineage of spiritual masters extending back to prehistory, is our human link with the original initiator, the Supreme Lord himself.

As anyone who's tried practicing a mantra they learned

from a book or overheard in a class knows, such a mantra has no "juice." But when we "plug in" to the lineage of enlightenment through the "outlet" of a human guru, we receive a living mantra charged with the blessing force of the guru tradition. Pandit Tigunait was able to intuit the mantras because his spiritual master had authorized him to do so. Without the active consent of the living tradition he never would have known what mantras to give, and the mantras he did pass on to Brunette would have lacked spiritual potency.

The guru is not a person; it's the flow of illuminating power which is the basis of spiritual life. Not everyone needs a human guru; some great masters in the twentieth century (such as Anandamayi Ma, Ramana Maharshi, and Ammachi) have been "self-illumined." But as anyone who's tried to start a campfire in the woods by rubbing two sticks together knows, things move a lot more quickly when someone whose fire is already alight brings you over a burning fagot.

Grappling with the Guru

So is the human guru a fallible person, or a divine being? Spiritual aspirants have struggled with this question for millennia. Many early Christians (such as the Arians and Nestorians) believed Jesus was a specially chosen, particularly pure human being through whom the spirit of God manifested. Others believed he was literally part of the Godhead himself, and some of them even claimed that although his contemporaries could see him, he was so pure he didn't really have a physical body!

According to the yoga tradition there is a wide spectrum of types of realized beings, ranging from actual incarnations of God, called *avatars*, to "part-time" masters. Look at it this way: when you see a particularly good movie, you completely forget that you exist, becoming totally identified with the characters in the film. Just so, we have forgotten we are travelers from another world who will move on to yet another world after this one; instead we've become completely identified with the drama going on around us on planet Earth. A "part-time" master is one who remembers who he really is for some length of time, but then slips back into the melodrama. He vacillates between enlightened awareness and ordinary human consciousness. A "full-time" master has stabilized herself in the illumined state and is no longer fooled by the images flickering on the screen of her awareness. Our guru may be any one of these types, or may simply be another person much like ourselves who happens to be walking a little further ahead of us along the path.

Just as there are different levels of teachers, so are there different styles of teaching. Some gurus want you to follow their instructions implicitly. Others deliberately send you false signals in order to wean you from dependence on them. Swami Rama did this constantly. Once he told Devi to pass along to a friend some advice that Devi knew was disastrous, involving marrying a man her friend didn't love. Ever the trusting disciple, Devi obeyed. Her friend had the good sense not to follow the bad advice, so Swamiji sent Devi to her again with the same message. The third time Swamiji told her to go speak with her friend, Devi finally objected, "I can't do this, Swamiji. What we're telling her is wrong."

"You finally got it!" Swamiji roared. At last Devi realized that Swami Rama wasn't interested in turning her into an automaton—he wanted her to trust her own inner guidance, to become a master in her own right, not a mindless disciple.

According to the yoga tradition the first quality a disciple requires is *viveka*, discrimination. We need to use our discriminating intelligence to discern authentic spiritual masters rooted in divine awareness from would-be gurus firmly established in self-delusion and egotism. And we need to use our clearest judgment to identify when a guru figure may be doing something we feel is seriously wrong, and to discuss our reservations honestly with him or her. "The worst crime," Swamiji always said, "is to kill your conscience."

Lighting the Lamp of Sadhana

Pandit Tigunait told me there are two times we must have a guru: at the very beginning, to set us on the path; and at the very end, to receive us into the state of enlightenment. In between the guru can do little for us except keep us inspired. We have to do our *sadhana*, spiritual practice, for ourselves—not even an avatar can do it for us. For those of us yoga students in the West, sadhana consists primarily of meditation *(dhyana)* and selfless service *(karma yoga)*. Cultivating meditation and managing our karma are the twin themes I'll be discussing in this book, sharing insights I've gleaned from the yoga masters I've been privileged to study with over the years.

As I travel around the country these days talking with yoga students, the single most common complaint I hear is, "My spiritual practices don't seem to be getting me anywhere. It's hard to stay motivated." Let's have a look at what's causing this problem and what the yogis say we can do about it. Let's also review why we started meditating in the first place and take a fresh look at where an enlivened spiritual practice is going to take us. For readers new to meditation, or who've been on vacation from their practice for a while, the last chapter offers a quick description of how yoga students shift gears from ordinary waking consciousness into the meditative state.

chapter two

The Unknown Ocean: Exploring Your Inner Depths

I DIDN'T BELIEVE my husband when he told me there had been a tribe of American Indians living twenty miles from the Oregon coast who didn't know the Pacific Ocean existed. "That can't be true!" I scoffed.

"They were studied by anthropologists in the 1800s. There was a ridge between them and the coast so they'd never actually seen the ocean. They had everything they needed in the valley where they lived, so they didn't bother traveling beyond their ancestral territory. This is a true story," Johnathan insisted. "It's documented."

Frankly I'm still not sure I believe him, but stranger things have happened. Imagine how the first yoga teachers arriving in the United States must have felt—great teachers like Swami Vivekananda and Paramahansa Yogananda and Rama Tirtha—when they found that most Americans had no idea that a vast inner world exists beyond their everyday thoughts. People born in Western culture recognize basically three states of awareness: either we're awake, or we're asleep, or we're watching TV. How difficult it must have been for the meditation masters to communicate about the intensely lucid states of consciousness yogis experience during their inner exploration to Westerners who are completely unaware that an ocean of awareness exists just over the ridge of their mental chatter.

The Native American tribe would have had to travel only twenty miles to discover an expanse of water vast beyond their imagination; but we don't have to take a single step—all we have to do is sit still, close our eyes, and pay attention—to uncover a whole new dimension of reality. Very few Westerners, however, have the interest or the patience to pause for a moment and look inside—yet inner explorers of every mystical tradition have promised that if we do so we will find guidance, serenity, and the source of healing and creative power.

When such extraordinary inner resources are available to those who travel inward, why do many of us feel such intense resistance to daily meditation? What does the yoga tradition recommend to help us overcome the obstacles which prevent us from discovering our inner world? What techniques are offered for attaining the yogic level of concentration necessary to travel deep within? And what happens when we uncover our inner light?

Surprisingly few Americans are attracted to meditation. Perhaps this is because we are emphatically conditioned to ignore our inner states. The first year I practiced meditation I constantly fought the sense that I was wasting time, that I ought to get up and do something. Our culture is oriented toward action, not toward inner reflection. In fact at times it seems as if it is explicitly constructed to shield us from our inner reality; instead of introducing us to our inner core, it keeps us continually distracted and preoccupied. We've become so divorced from ourselves that we actually believe there's nothing inside us that is particularly interesting or valuable; so rather than meditating, most people spend their free time watching TV, gossiping, or getting intoxicated.

Not even our religions teach us how to commune with our innermost spirit, and the resulting inner emptiness is poignant. Over the past few years I've spent many hours in a cancer unit at a major American hospital. On the oncology ward there is a separate TV for each individual patient. The TV in the waiting room is never turned off; there are even TVs in the exam rooms. Some of the patients there are facing imminent death, yet the best modern medicine can offer is distraction—game shows and soap operas and violent movies. In the face of death itself no one is encouraged to dive within and make contact with their immortal spirit. Patients pass away as *The Dating Game* blares from a screen above their heads.

What distinguishes yoga students from most other people is that we've learned to value inner stillness; we sincerely want to find our innermost self. This is why we make a commitment to meditation practice. But once outer distractions are overcome, an internal set of obstacles arises which make deep levels of meditation difficult to achieve.

Turning Off Our Inner Light

Most of us in the West, who don't have the advantage of having an enlightened spiritual mentor on the premises to continually inspire us, bring a weak level of intensity to our spiritual practice. And so, not surprisingly, the door to deeper levels of concentration seems jammed shut. Rather than experiencing illuminating inner states, we experience the nine impediments to the fulfillment of our practice described in the sage Patanjali's classic *Yoga Sutra*, compiled around the second century B.C. Fortunately each of these problems can be overcome if we're sincere about making progress in our inner exploration.

1. Unfitness. Contrary to popular belief, meditation is not for everyone. The yoga scriptures specify that meditation should be taught only to those students who exhibit emotional equipoise, psychological maturity, intelligence, the ability to concentrate, strong personal ethics, and high motivation. Meditation can actually be detrimental for those who are emotionally unbalanced, and it may serve only to strengthen negative qualities in people who are hostile or arrogant.

Antidote. Those who are not yet qualified for meditative practice are encouraged to prepare themselves by practicing karma yoga first. Traditionally this means cultivating selfless service (helping others without expecting any reward) and performing religious observances. The physical gestures and psychological associations of ritual practice help focus the mind and purify the heart.

2. Doubt. If we have not met adepts who've attained the goal of yoga—liberation from the bonds of birth and death—we may not really feel the full liberating potential of yoga in our gut. Or we may find it hard to believe that although others could achieve a state of illumination, that state is available to us too.

Antidote. Spending time in the presence of great souls is the most powerful cure for doubt. The masters show us by their living example that yoga really works. I've never met a saint who had patience for our crippling belief that, unlike them, we can't possibly attain something great. Saints unfailingly see the divine potential in us and expect us to see it too. One drawback to this antidote is that some students approach the sages with completely unrealistic expectations, and when they discover that even the greatest saints are still human beings, another round of doubt sets in. See the saints for what they are, not for what you expect them to be. Revere the light coming through them, but also acknowledge their humanity.

3. Laziness. Inertia (*tamas*) is one of the three fundamental forces in yoga cosmology. It arises when the body or mind feels "heavy." Nothing keeps the soul chained to the cycle of birth and death more effectively than the refusal to rouse oneself and take charge of one's spiritual destiny.

Antidote. Sloth is counteracted by self-discipline, and self-discipline is maintained by enthusiasm for spiritual practice. As the yogis say, *tamas* is overcome by *rajas*, the principle of activity, energy, dynamic will, the second fundamental force. When *rajas* is guided by the third force, *sattva*, harmony, light, or enlightened understanding, then rapid spiritual progress becomes possible.

4. Illness. Most of us know how difficult it is to concentrate when we're feeling ill. For people who are sick a lot, this can create a major obstacle to their spiritual growth.

Antidote. Eating health-giving foods, exercising regularly, maintaining a hatha yoga regimen, practicing cleansing yogic techniques like *nadi shodhanam* (alternate nostril breathing) or the nasal wash, and keeping a positive mental attitude can go a long way toward preventing physical disorders from taking over our consciousness. Consulting an adept health practitioner who understands the dynamics of the vital force, such as a homeopath, Ayurvedic physician, or acupuncturist, can help correct imbalanced subtle energies which may be creating disturbances in our meditation.

5. Self-delusion. There is a not-so-subtle distinction between the subconscious and the superconscious which beginning yoga students sometimes miss. When the *tattvas*, or subtle elements, play across their mental screen during meditation, students who haven't learned to differentiate between the images cast up by their imagination and the genuine promptings of spirit often get confused. They may mistakenly believe they are having divinely inspired visions, that their kundalini is rising, or that they're receiving psychic guidance from supernatural beings or are under psychic attack by unseen forces.

Antidote. Swami Rama repeatedly emphasized that whenever we either see or hear anything in meditation, we must "let it go." Whether it be nagging thoughts and fantasies, or seemingly spectacular sights and sounds and revelations, "let it go." The realm we are trying to make contact with in meditation is formless; there are no sights or sounds there in the sense that we commonly understand. He urged us to recognize that any meditative experience that inflates our ego (from "I had a clairvoyant experience!" to "I saw God!") is not a good meditative result. A successful meditation for beginning-level students is one which leaves us in a lucid, refreshed, tranquil state.

6. Craving. Sensuality *(kama)* and desire for the good things in life *(artha)* have their place in the yoga tradition, but meditation is not one such place. If one is so preoccupied by desires for material success and pleasure that he or she cannot stop thinking about them even during meditation, spiritual success is not likely to occur.

Antidote. By surrendering the spirit of greediness, one transcends one's cravings. In India many yogis and yoginis visualize themselves offering the material objects they desire to God or the Goddess, surrendering the gifts of material life back to the supreme giver. Learning to let go of the things we crave so much that they're creating obstacles in our meditation requires the development of discriminating knowledge—continual awareness of the comparative value of transient things versus lasting spiritual attainments. It is necessary for us to let go of the world of the senses so that we can enter the world beyond our senses, as the yoga texts explain.

7. Incorrect Understanding. How many yoga classes have you attended in which, after the teacher has clearly explained how to breathe diaphragmatically, silently, and without jerks or pauses, at least one student continues to breathe so noisily and erratically the entire class can hear it? The student may be sincere, but he or she has simply not understood the instructions. For those of us who are developing the concentration skills necessary to deepen our meditation, correctly understanding the yogic processes involved is imperative. Entering the inner world, there are many places we can go astray if our comprehension is mistaken or incomplete.

Antidote. Someone who aspires to be a competent yoga student must have a competent teacher, and definitely must attend carefully to what the teacher is saying. Students progress by applying and testing what they've learned, and then returning to their mentor for correction and further guidance.

8. Not Achieving Results. One of the most common complaints of beginning yoga aspirants is that their meditative practice doesn't appear to be going anywhere. Students become discouraged, give up, or content themselves with meaningless, mechanical practice if they don't see quick results from their meditation.

Antidote. Vyasa, an ancient master who wrote a famous commentary on the *Yoga Sutra*, explains that not attaining the results of meditative practice means one is not properly established in the practice. If the practice is performed properly, with full attention, its benefits must appear. If a student feels that he or she is getting nowhere with meditation, it is important to seek guidance from a teacher who has mastered the states the student is making an effort to achieve. Experienced teachers can often instantly identify an unconscious habit pattern that may be sabotaging the student's sincere efforts.

9. Not Maintaining Results. Perhaps the most common complaint of intermediate-level yoga aspirants is that the results they achieve from meditation appear inconsistent. The student may have a series of excellent meditations, then for several days in a row have trouble concentrating. An inability to consistently return to the higher states of concentration can be terribly frustrating for a serious meditator.

Antidote. After all these years I can still feel Swami Rama's advice ringing in my ears: "Practice, practice, practice! Practice makes perfect!" Learning to walk or to ride a bike took practice too—you may have fallen down a few times, but eventually you learned to balance. Remaining balanced in higher meditative states also takes practice; for those of us Westerners entirely unaccustomed to inner life, it may take a lot of practice! Anyone who wants to achieve a great goal—whether it's becoming an Olympic-level athlete, a doctor, or an accomplished artist—has to face years of hard work before achieving mastery. Reaching enlightenment is the greatest goal of all, and it's reserved for those who "Practice, practice, practice!"

Swami Hariharananda Aranya, one of the greatest Sankhya masters of the twentieth century, had some encouraging words for aspirants struggling with this problem. He explained that "through special devotion to God" the mind becomes increasingly *sattvic* (pure, harmonious, full of light), which makes maintaining higher states of awareness easier and easier.

These nine impediments, set forth in *Yoga Sutra* 1:30, keep the door to inner perception closed tight. By sincerely applying the antidotes we can pry open that door and peer into the inner worlds. Sutra 1:20 advises all yoga practitioners to apply reverent faith and enthusiastic effort in achieving this aim. By continually remembering our goal, concentrating one-pointedly, and developing discriminating knowledge, we unlock the gateway leading to our higher self. Sutra 1:21 promises that students who persevere with an intense degree of devotion and determination will quickly reach the goal.

Intensity of Focus

Strong determination leads to intensity of focus in meditation, the one-pointedness that opens the door to knowledge of our higher self. But what does it actually mean to be one-pointed?

You may recall that several years ago undetected weaknesses in the wall of a jetliner caused its fuselage to abruptly rip apart while the plane was in the air. The passengers seated near the shattered wall were pulled into the plane's engines, and any flight personnel who weren't buckled into a seat at the moment of the explosion were sucked out the gaping hole in the side of the jet, plummeting thousands of feet to their deaths. In the cockpit the pilot struggled to keep the mangled plane from crashing. He was in his mid-sixties; this was to have been his next-to-last flight before retiring. What this meant for the terrified passengers was that the most experienced pilot in the entire airline was at the helm of that jet. Against unimaginable odds, he managed to land the plane safely.

In an interview the next day reporters wanted to know what had been going through the pilot's mind as he fought to keep the plane in the air till he reached a safe landing site. Was he thinking of the hundreds of passengers for whose lives he was responsible? Did he think about his wife and grandchildren? Was he haunted by the prospect of dying at any moment in a fiery crash? The pilot admitted that none of these things—not even the possibility of his own death—had crossed his mind. From the second the plane lurched out of control till the moment it rolled to a stop on the runway, only one thought played across the field of his awareness. "I was thinking about flying that plane," he said.

Great yoga masters bring this same level of absolutely one-pointed focus to their meditation practice. Aware that at any moment death can remove us from this plane of reality, the masters focus with keen motivation and self-disciplined intensity. When we can achieve the same intensity of focus that pilot displayed, we begin to experience our inner light.

Yoga science offers eight powerful techniques to help us attain a concentrated inward focus.

1. Morality. Nothing disturbs one's meditation like a guilty conscience. The spiritual masters ask us to renounce harming others, lying, stealing, overindulging in physical pleasures, and greed.

2. Ethics. Instead of hurting others, the yoga masters ask us to cultivate physical and mental purity, contentment, self-control, spiritual studies, and devotion. These increase the sattva, the quality of light, in our mental field, and calm our emotions.

3. Posture. The *Yoga Sutra* advises us to sit upright in a comfortable and relaxed position when we prepare to meditate. Anyone who has experimented with different postures immediately senses the improved clarity of consciousness when he or she sits up straight. The nervous system operates maximally when the body is in this position.

4. Breath. The connection between the breath and the mind is so close that a person breathing erratically is unmistakably thinking erratically, while a person whose breath is calm also enjoys a calm mind. When the breath is slow, smooth, and gentle, the *sushumna*, or central nerve channel of the subtle body, is activated, and one begins to breathe equally through both nostrils. The mind becomes clear and tranquil.

5. Sense Withdrawal. Releasing one's awareness of the body and breath, the meditator relaxes into pure awareness. At this point consciousness is completely interiorized, serene, and lucid.

6. Concentration. Here the mind is focused on a mental object such as a mantra, a light, or the image of a deity. Each time the mind wanders away, one gently brings it back to the mental object. This exercise is more difficult than it appears, so it helps to have an object in which one has great faith, such as a mantra given by a realized master or the image of a god, goddess, or saint one particularly loves.

7. Meditation. When one's attention flows uninterruptedly toward an inner object, he or she is in a state of meditation.

8. Superconsciousness. There comes a state in meditative absorption in which the mental distinction between oneself and the object one is focusing on disappears. All that appears to exist is a unified field of consciousness. This is the state of intense focus toward which all yogis aspire. According to the *Yoga Sutra*, this state leads to extraordinary mental powers and finally to enlightenment itself.

Yogis move seamlessly from concentration into meditation and on into the superconscious state called samadhi. Patanjali calls this threefold process *samyama*. Concentration, the first stage of samyama, is much like a plane lifting off: the pilot focuses intently on each detail involved in getting the jetliner safely off the ground. In the second stage, meditation, the pilot guides the plane higher into the sky. In the third stage, samadhi, the pilot cruises effortlessly at 30,000 feet. On the ground it would require the pilot an hour and a half to drive 100 miles, but in her aircraft thousands of feet above the Earth she travels that distance in minutes. Samyama gives the yogi the ability to travel mentally at speeds unknown to ordinary human awareness, since time and space as we know them cannot follow the meditator into the highest levels of samadhi.

The *Yoga Sutra* lists all kinds of exciting abilities one can develop in the superconscious state, from knowledge of one's past lives, to clairvoyance, to levitation. But the most important skill one can acquire is the ability to distinguish between *buddhi sattva* and *purusha*, that is, between the subtlemost portion of the mind and the immortal soul, between the lower self and the higher self. When one's awareness is established in the higher self rather than identified with the nonstop traffic of thoughts and feelings careening through the mind, he or she gains immortality because the higher self doesn't die. It exists outside time and space in the inner light of pure awareness.

Going into the Light

All spiritual traditions speak of the light within. The *Maitri Upanishad* says that after passing through the inner light the yogi attains the supreme goal of yoga. The well-known *gayatri* mantra, repeated daily by most spiritual aspirants in India, is designed to invoke this light. It says, "We meditate on the divine inner sun, the most splendid light in all the worlds. Please illuminate our minds!" The mantra is petitioning the higher self to shine its wisdom and healing power into the *buddhi sattva*, the purest part of our everyday consciousness.

Some people literally see light during this experience. Many individuals who've had near-death experiences report that while they were clinically dead, they saw an intensely bright light. Often they claim that it was the most ecstatic moment of their lives, as they bathed in this brilliant light that radiated love, healing, wisdom, and guidance. Indeed, the purpose of yoga is to live and die in the light of the higher self.

The holiest city in India is called Varanasi because the Varana River marks its northern border, while a creek called Asi marks the southern end. The sacred Ganges River flows along the city's eastern shore. But from time immemorial Varanasi has also been called Kashi, "the City of Light." Hindus aspire to die in Varanasi since, according to legend, anyone who dies within its precincts automatically achieves liberation. Lord Shiva is said to be eternally present in this city, and to instantly release those who pass out of their bodies here from the chains of birth and death.

According to the yoga tradition this is actually true. But one needs to understand that the Varana River is *pingala*, the right nerve current in the subtle body, and that the Asi is *ida*, the left current. The Ganges is *sushumna*, the central channel through which kundalini travels upwards from the bottom of the spine toward the top of the head in deep states of meditation. The yogis explain that the City of Light is your *sahasrara* chakra, the center of awareness associated with the uppermost portion of your brain. This is where Lord Shiva, the deity who represents the supreme consciousness, resides. At death, whether you are in Varanasi or Venice, London or Los Angeles, if you can hold your full awareness in this divine inner city Lord Shiva will instantly liberate you. Yogis aim to remain fully conscious during the process of death, with their attention intently focused in the sahasrara chakra, the inner Varanasi.

But you can't die in Varanasi unless you live there. And living in the City of Light means learning to meditate with full concentration, sincerity, and devotion. Meditation is an inner adventure, a path into worlds our five senses cannot show us. Not everyone is a born explorer, but for those of us who are drawn to the adventure of inner life, the universe within, mapped by the great masters, is constantly beckoning.

Within each of us is an unknown ocean of consciousness. It has no shore—majestic and tranquil, it extends forever. Like the tribe of Native Americans on the Oregon coast who never saw the sea, we can be content to live in our present little enclave, bounded by our five senses. Or we can draw in our senses, focus our attention, and set sail into an ocean of light.

chapter three

Meditation Is Boring

I WAS ARGUING WITH Swami Rama, as usual. He had called me aside to discuss my meditation practice, and he clearly didn't understand what I was saying. Swamiji was insisting that I focus my awareness at my heart center. Since I had recently graduated from college at the top of my class, I was surprised that he failed to recognize that, due to my towering intellect, obviously I should concentrate at my *ajña* chakra, the center in the brain behind the eyebrows.

Barely concealing his exasperation, Swamiji pointed to my head. "That," he said emphatically, "is yours. This"— he pointed to my heart—"is mine."

I went home and reluctantly sat down on my meditation cushion. The truth was, I didn't enjoy meditating. It was a tedious chore, one sure way to make twenty minutes drag on for what seemed like hours. I thought of myself as an expert on meditation—I could recite the nine impediments to success in yoga practice and their antidotes for you at the drop of a nickel—but I hated to meditate. I would much rather read about meditation—about its numerous well-documented physical, psychological, and spiritual benefits—than actually do it. It was boring.

Unenthusiastically, I tried to bring my awareness to my heart region. It was amazingly difficult. I was so completely entrenched in my head that redirecting my attention even as far downward as my neck required real effort. And when I did manage to concentrate on my heart, the feeling was extremely uncomfortable. Anger and old resentments continuously bubbled into my awareness. My heart felt like a clogged toilet, filled with all kinds of ugly material I didn't want to smell.

I struggled on for months, trying to follow my meditation schedule faithfully, resisting the temptation to keep glancing at my watch to see if it was finally time to get up. Even when I seemed to reach a space of quiet clarity, in a nanosecond a thought would arise and I'd lose myself in reverie before I even realized what had happened. Then I'd catch myself, force the image out of my mind, and return to the monotonous drone of my mantra.

One day Pandit Tigunait invited me to his home. As he spoke about the Supreme Being (who, like many other Hindus, he visualized as the Mother of the Universe), his face began to glow. It surprised me to hear such a brilliant intellectual speak of the Divine Mother with so much innocent devotion. But that evening as I sat down to meditate I remembered how in my childhood I would pray every night with innocent faith similar to his. And for the first time in years I inwardly turned to the Divine Being as if it were a living, caring reality rather than a divine abstraction.

It was one of the most extraordinary moments of my life. My heart blew open and wave upon wave of ecstasy swept through my consciousness. I sat in bliss for hours, never wanting to get up.

After this my attitude toward meditation completely changed. Sitting became the highlight of my life. I could hardly wait for the twice-daily meditation sessions scheduled at the ashram where I lived, and would slip off whenever I could find a few free moments to enjoy the rapture of inner communion. I was humbled now to realize how insightful Swami Rama's original analysis had been: that I needed to get out of my head, clear the debris out of my heart, and open myself to the stream of divine love.

At this point I honestly believed I had made it to Easy Street, and from here on all I needed to do was coast effortlessly toward enlightenment. Then one morning I sat down to meditate and, to my utter bewilderment, my inner attunement had completely disappeared. My heart felt dry as brick and my mind kept getting distracted. After struggling with this for several days I went to Pandit Tigunait and complained, "Overnight, for no reason I can tell, I've lost the ability to focus. I was having intense experiences of inner joy, and now they're gone!"

Panditji's response surprised me. He explained that *ananda* (inner bliss) pulsates outward from the higher self in waves, and that sincere aspirants must stick with their daily practice during both the peaks and the troughs. He also suggested that I was becoming too attached to the sensation of bliss, that there are many far higher states, and that I needed to move on in my inner exploration. He advised me to continue cultivating devotion, but not to lose sight of important fundamental techniques such as breath awareness to quiet the mind.

Over the ensuing years, through many more ups and downs of meditative experience, I sought out advanced practitioners to ask what methods they use to get them through the dry periods. I also asked what techniques yoga masters use to inspire beginning students, who, after the initial burst of enthusiasm for practice wears off, sometimes find their meditation becoming lifeless. Fortunately the yoga tradition offers many methods for keeping interest high during that challenging period before our practice begins to bear fruit and we can actually see the concrete results of our inner efforts.

Satsanga

The one universally acclaimed method of keeping one's spiritual practice enlivened is *satsanga*, which literally means "keeping the company of truth." The easiest and most effective way to do this is to spend as much time as possible in the presence of one's guru or other saints. For those of us in America, where saints sometimes seem to be in short supply, this isn't always practical. Here, satsanga has more often come to mean spending time with our fellow aspirants, so that working together or meditating together or even simply socializing, we can support each other spiritually and keep one another inspired.

There are two ways to keep company with the saints themselves, however, even when they're not physically present. The first is to keep pictures of our guru and the other masters of our tradition on our altar or in our heart. According to the yogis, the lineage of teachers is actually a living energy field, called *guru shakti*, and we can contact that transmission of enlightening force when we still our minds and focus on the guru within. When we sincerely surrender to the living voice of our yogic lineage it provides continual guidance and inspiration both in our practice and in the ordinary affairs of daily life.

A year or so ago I had a serious health crisis, and for the first time in my life I had to be taken to the emergency room. The doctors ran a battery of tests to check my heart, then sent me home to rest while they awaited the results. As I lay in bed, quite shaken up, I found myself calling out to my spiritual mentor, "Panditji, wherever you are, please help me!"

The phone started ringing. "Linda, I am feeling you very close. How are you doing?" I could hardly believe it was really Panditji, who many years before had accepted me as his spiritual daughter and initiated me in the tradition of the Great Goddess. This experience confirmed for me that once we embark on spiritual life, we are all linked in subtle, extraordinary ways, and that the masters of the lineage continually hold us in the field of their awareness, whether we know it or not.

The second way to enjoy satsanga is to read about the lives of the saints and to study their teachings. The example of how they lived and the wisdom they shared with those around them constitute their enduring legacy. Reading about great spiritual masters is no substitute for actually having a living guru or other spiritual elders in our lives, but it will keep the flames of faith and spiritual determination burning when the guru is physically absent.

Bhakti

In the early 1970s an influx of tremendously influential teachers from India, including Swami Rama and Maharishi Mahesh Yogi, inspired an entire generation to explore yoga. They took great pains to emphasize the scientific nature of yoga, maintaining that one did not need to adopt Hinduism in order to practice meditation. In taking care to respect the religious sensibilities of Westerners, however, the deeply devotional aspects of yoga as it is actually practiced in India were de-emphasized. Some of us launched into yoga without appreciating how important *bhakti*—devotion—truly is on the spiritual path. Others of us may even have projected onto our spiritual teachers a level of devotion that might more appropriately have been directed toward God. Swami Rama would quickly get fed up when would-be disciples fawned before him, and often shouted, "Don't worship me! Worship God!"

According to the tantric tradition, the Divine Being loves us so much that it assumes any form we imagine God to be in, and comes to us in that form. This is the reason yogis are not interested in converting anyone. They feel that the Divine Being works through the form of Jesus as well as of Krishna or Buddha or the Divine Mother. In India gurus often assign an *ishta devata*, or personal deity, to their disciples, based on the disciple's history and inclinations. For many Westerners this might be Jesus, Yahweh, Mary, or Allah. The disciple then cultivates a deep personal relationship with God or the Goddess in that form, and regularly engages in prayer and worship. In this way the spiritual path ceases to be an abstract quest for an intangible absolute, and becomes a form of joyous communion with the higher self of all beings.

Ammachi, a contemporary saint from South India, says that spiritual practice without devotion is "like eating stones." Many saints claim that developing a loving relationship with the Divine is the quickest of all spiritual paths. In meditation we still our mind so that we can feel the living presence of our beloved deity beside us and inside us.

Karma Yoga

Too often beginning yoga students have the sense that when they're sitting in meditation they're doing their spiritual work, but when they get up and resume their external responsibilities they're now engaged in "mere" worldly activities. This is not the yogic perspective. In the *Bhagavad Gita* Krishna strongly emphasizes the importance of karma yoga, or yoga in action. "Fix your mind on the higher self rather than the lower ego," he tells us, "and dedicate all your actions to God. This will free you from the bondage of karma."

If sitting in meditation represents our inner study, then getting up and dealing with our relatives, our boss, and the entire menagerie of people around us is our practicum. Here is where we are able to see if our practice has "taken," and to "apply" the sense of serenity and objectivity meditation has given us. Meditation becomes more interesting when we begin recognizing its effects in our daily life, and using the clarity it helps us achieve in practical situations. Meditation is not something "other" than life, but something that should be carried over into life, helping us maintain a comparatively stress-free state through all the normally stressful events of the day.

Bodhi Chitta

An aspect of meditation practice strongly emphasized in Buddhist forms of yoga is the cultivation of *bodhi chitta*, loving-kindness. Hindus also often conclude their meditations with chants such as Loka *samastha sukhino bhavantu*, "May all beings in all worlds be well!" When we meditate we're not merely inching toward enlightenment; much more is happening on subtle levels. Every time we create a space of peaceful clarity in ourselves we are helping to purify the polluted psychic atmosphere of our planet. When a student asked why the great yoga masters in the Himalayas don't come down out of the mountains to help humanity, Swami Rama insisted that the yogis sitting in their cave monasteries are doing more to protect and regenerate the world than hundreds of activists put together. For students who find it difficult to motivate themselves to sit for meditation consistently, it may be helpful to recognize that their practice not only benefits themselves but is also a form of service to the world. Cultivating stillness and clarity in meditation, and sending out one's good wishes to all other creatures in the universe, is a powerful way to begin developing the blessing force so characteristic of great saints. Meditation becomes a selfless gift, our offering for world peace.

Kirtan

An extremely popular way of keeping the level of inspiration high in India is *kirtan,* singing beautiful *bhajans* (religious songs) which elevate the spirit. From the haunting Bengali bhajans translated into English by Paramahansa Yogananda and sung at many of his U.S. centers, to the popular recordings of the musicians at Mount Madonna Center near Santa Cruz, to the exquisite chants favored at Siddha Yoga centers, devotional singing has caught on with many Western yoga groups, and is often used as a prelude to meditation.

Singing opens the heart and focuses the mind; the mantras and sacred names of God incorporated in many bhajans prepare the soul for going inward. Singing, playing, or listening to spiritually charged music can dramatically alter one's mood, creating a sacred atmosphere highly conducive to spiritual practice. Beautiful melodies and meaningful lyrics transport us almost effortlessly into a meditative state.

Pranayama

When I was first learning to meditate, Swami Rama constantly emphasized the importance of breath control (pranayama), much to my disgust. As he launched into yet another lecture on alternate nostril breathing, I would impatiently wonder when he was finally going to give us the real yoga techniques. It took me years to realize that practices like diaphragmatic breathing, breath awareness, and alternate nostril breathing are the real techniques. In the beginning I never bothered to practice them conscientiously because they were so simple that I just couldn't believe they would have much effect. But when I finally sat down and began working consciously with my breath, I was astounded by the profound impact these exercises had on my awareness. As Swamiji often repeated, "Breath is the flywheel of life," giving us direct access to departments of our nervous system usually beyond our conscious control.

The late Kashmiri master Swami Lakshmanjoo strongly emphasized the importance of maintaining sandhi, "the center between two breaths." When the breath becomes extremely refined, flowing gently and equally through both nostrils rather than predominantly through one or the other, a deep sense of peace is attained. When this is held with "continuously refreshed awareness which is achieved through devotion to the Lord," one attains real spiritual experience. But "this state of concentration can be achieved only after you have freed your mind of all worldly cares, completed your daily routine activities, and have had your full amount of sleep. . . . Your mind must be serene, free from the forced obligation to meditate, determined with devotion to discover God consciousness."

Lakshmanjoo also sternly warned, "If you undergo these practices for one thousand centuries without full awareness and concentration, you will have wasted all one thousand of those centuries. The movement of breath has to be filled with full awareness and concentration." Smooth, even, diaphragmatic breathing, without jerks or pauses, is the gentle wind that propels the sailboat of our mind into the calm lake of meditation.

Hatha Yoga

For centuries many yogis and yoginis in India have turned to hatha yoga postures to prepare themselves for meditation. Practicing yoga asanas helps keep the body healthy, the muscles supple, and the back strong and steady so that one can sit in meditation for extended periods of time. But asanas also have a powerful effect on one's mental state, fostering the clear and relaxed frame of mind so conducive to meditation. While aerobic exercises strongly energize the body and mind, giving you the heart-pumping sense that you're ready to tackle the world, yoga exercises energize in a more subtle way, leaving you feeling calm but alert.

The first time I experienced this was after a particularly excellent hatha class. I felt so wonderful I was practically unable to leave the yoga center! It seemed to me that if I stepped outdoors I'd float up to the clouds before reaching the parking lot; in fact, it felt a lot like being in heaven already. Then I noticed that, as a result of having performed a series of yoga postures and the concluding relaxation exercise with full attention and in a tranquil and balanced fashion, both my nostrils were flowing freely. I was breathing exactly as Swami Rama recommended students breathe as they begin their meditation:

slowly, evenly, diaphragmatically, without any jerks or pauses in the breath. He called the state where both nostrils flow freely, quietly, and smoothly "sushumna awakening," meaning that the subtle energy channels in the region of the spine are activated in a spiritually charged manner, creating a state he called "joyous mind." I sat down and meditated for half an hour, taking advantage of the extraordinary sense of clarity and serenity I was experiencing.

Meditators who are drawn to physical practices often find that performing a balanced series of yoga postures automatically delivers them to a meditative state.

Puja

For most of my life there was scarcely anything I could think of more tedious than rituals. I had sat through too many utterly lifeless religious ceremonies as a child to ever want anything to do with these types of rites again. I couldn't fathom how Swami Satyananda from our local Kali temple could be so enthusiastic about *pujas*, rituals in which flowers, incense, grains, and other objects are offered to the Divine Mother. (Yes, there is a real temple to the warrior goddess Kali in my neighborhood. I live in California.)

One day Swami Satyananda finally persuaded me to join in a puja with him, and the experience turned out to be remarkable. This particular puja was quite elaborate, involving chanting a long litany of mantras while making offerings to a sacred fire. Chanting mantras out loud automatically regulated my breath, while focusing on the unfamiliar Sanskrit words concentrated my mind sharply. There was instant feedback if my concentration slipped: I would mispronounce a mantra. By the end of the ritual my mind was so one-pointed I was already in meditation.

Less elaborate pujas can also be a valuable way to create

a powerful meditative atmosphere. Place a photo or statue of the deity you love, or of saints you feel attracted to, or of the teachers in your guru lineage on your meditation altar. A symbolic picture of the Divine such as the cross, Sri Yantra, or the word "Om" will do if you feel uncomfortable with anthropomorphic images. Create a sacred space around the altar by inviting your mind to accept that the Divine Being really is present in the image you've selected. Then offer flowers, bits of food, or incense to the living presence of the Divine you feel in the image. You may wish to wave a lighted candle in a circle before the picture or statue, as yogis sometimes do in a ceremony called *arati*. Finally, sincerely offer the reverence in your heart. Having established a sense of sacred communion, sit quietly and begin your meditation.

In India orthodox families offer a portion of their meals to the images on their meditation altars before eating. This is said to sanctify the food.

Punctuality

Being regular in one's meditation practice is also tremendously helpful. At the ashram where I lived we all meditated together at 6 a.m. and 10 p.m. every day without fail. For the first few weeks I would sit down and consciously regulate my breath. But as the rhythm of regular meditation became a deeply ingrained habit, I found that the moment I sat on my cushion, my breath spontaneously became very subtle and my mind stilled. I no longer had to work at entering a meditative state—my body automatically entered that state at the appropriate time. It was as if I had two daily appointments with the Divine Mother. I would walk into the meditation room and she would be waiting for me and sweep me into her arms. I didn't have to make any effort at all.

Lakshmanjoo used to remind his students never to think of meditation as a chore. "When you are about to meditate you must feel excitement and be thankful to God that you have received this opportunity. Unless you fall in love with meditation and approach it with total enthusiasm, you cannot enter the deeper realms of awareness."

There is one important point every meditator must understand: if you are bored, you are not meditating. Meditation cannot be boring, because meditation is, by definition, intense mental absorption, and intense concentration obliterates not only boredom but even the sense of time and space. Meditation is not only helpful in unlocking creativity and overcoming stress, it is the key to the inner dimensions of our spirit. By persevering in our meditation practice with determination, devotion, and enthusiasm, we unlock the door to the highest and best part of ourselves, and consciously enter the living depths of our immortal being. We enter samadhi, the superconscious state.

chapter four

Samadhi: Knowing It When You See It

A SAGE ABSORBED IN samadhi is a sight to see. I was sitting down with Swami Rama for dinner one evening when he paused to silently say thanks for our meal. Famished, I waited impatiently for him to finish so we could begin eating. Then I noticed that he had stopped breathing—he was as still and unmoving as a corpse. He was sitting bolt upright in his chair and still had good color in his cheeks—otherwise I would probably have called an ambulance.

I snuck up for a closer inspection, watching his chest for any sign of life. He was as inert as a rock. I slipped my fingers under his nose to check for any subtle current of air: this only confirmed that he definitely wasn't breathing. Swamiji had left the TV on, and coincidentally a program about airline pilots was playing. The screen showed an aircraft rising over the clouds and soaring tens of thousands of feet above the earth. I felt that Swami Rama was doing the same thing. He sat absolutely still for half an hour, absorbed in inner silence.

Some years later I was traveling through Bengal with Shree Maa, a remarkable yogini from Assam. One of her programs got out of hand: so many hundreds of devotees were pushing forward to ask for her blessing that it looked as if some people might be crushed in the melee. Abruptly Shree Maa, who was seated on a platform in front of the surging crowd, raised her right hand in blessing, closed her eyes, and passed into samadhi. She became completely still, yet the waves of peace emanating from her thin body enveloped the hall. Immediately the pushing, shouting crowd became still. It was amazing to see how her inner state affected everyone present.

In Calcutta I visited Swami Hariharananda Giri, one of the greatest living masters of kriya yoga. As he was answering my questions about yoga practice, a dozen or so of his close disciples silently arrived for the evening satsanga. Inviting my husband and me to join them, Hariharananda sat down on the floor near his students and slipped into samadhi. I meditated with the group for fifteen or twenty minutes till my curiosity about the kriya practitioners got the better of me. If I listened carefully I could hear myself and my husband breathing, but I couldn't hear any of the Indians at all—it was as if Johnathan and I were the only two people in the room. Sneaking a peek at the disciples sitting around me, I saw that they were all in samadhi, unmoving, unbreathing, absolutely still. After an hour and a half the session ended, and without a word the disciples bowed at the master's feet and left for home. Their total seriousness about spiritual practice and their ability to communicate with each other at the deepest levels without uttering a sound impressed me profoundly.

Yogis say samadhi is the door to superconscious states, the gateway to liberation. Many of us Western meditators don't seriously consider it a goal we're capable of attaining.

We aim instead for a few moments of relaxation and mental clarity simply to help us get through our busy, cluttered lives. The fantastic expansion of consciousness that can occur in samadhi seems unreal to us. We don't realize how close it is, just on the other side of our thoughts.

The Inner Stratosphere

Yoga is samadhi, the ancient yogic texts say. But what is samadhi? Most of us innocently begin yoga classes in hopes of improving our physical health and peace of mind. As we advance in our study and practice, however, we learn that *ashtanga* yoga, "the eight limbs of yoga," leads to a state of awareness called samadhi. Often we have the impression this is some incredibly elevated state of consciousness accessible only to the most advanced yogis, and that anyone who experiences it automatically becomes enlightened.

Because many yoga students have such serious misconceptions—about what samadhi is, about what they can and cannot accomplish through it, and about how it's achieved—let's review the perspectives offered by the yogis themselves.

First, samadhi is by no means one simple state. Patanjali's *Yoga Sutra* describes a gradient of five different levels of awareness:

1. Dissipated. This is our everyday state of mind, in which random thoughts flit incessantly from one subject to another. One minute we're promising ourselves we'll devote a full hour to our hatha yoga practice this morning, the next minute we're planning breakfast, and the next we're worrying about a project at work.

2. Stupefied. Sometimes the mind is hardly working at all. People who are drunk or sleepy (or watching TV!) are in this torpid state.

3. Distracted. The difference between this and the dissipated state is that, while in the latter we are completely unfocused, here there is some underlying point of attention from which our mind wanders. We may be preparing a report, or sitting quietly focusing on a mantra, when suddenly our mind is distracted by a noise outside the room or by a stray memory.

4. One-pointed. In this state, finally, we're really paying attention to what we're doing. We're focused completely in the present: breathing into a stretch in our hatha class, or wholly engaged in a conversation with a friend, or mentally working through a knotty problem. According to the scriptures, only those who can maintain this level of concentration are qualified to begin practicing yoga.

5. Absorbed. At this point the object of our awareness "swallows" our sense of self-consciousness—as, for example, when we completely forget ourselves and become the posture or the mantra. Nothing else exists in our awareness, not even our usual vivid sense of our own existence.

Samadhi occurs toward the top of this scale. Patanjali says there are two kinds of samadhi: *samprajñata*, superconsciousness with an object, which is a profoundly concentrated state in which thought and the sense of self persist; and *asamprajñata*, superconsciousness without an object, where the subject/object duality is completely transcended. Contrary to the popular conception that these states are far beyond the reach of the average person, almost every sincere meditator has already experienced the lower states of samprajñata samadhi, even if only for a moment. If you've been working with meditation, you may recognize some of them:

1. Unbroken concentration in which an external sense object (like a flame or a picture of a saint) is viewed intently within the mind. My husband seems to go into "computer samadhi" when he's on the Internet.

2. Unbroken concentration in which a "subtle" object (like an internal image of God or an inner sound or mantra) is held within the mind. Lovers who can't get their romantic partner out of their mind can hardly function because they're in this type of samadhi.

3. Unbroken concentration on the bliss within, in which the senses are completely withdrawn from any external or internal objects and are focused on themselves in a sort of ecstatic trance. We see this in the "rapture" and "beatitude" reported by our own Judeo-Christian mystics.

4. Unbroken concentration on our own existence, as in those incredibly lucid moments when we fully experience the reality that "I am."

Each of these four samadhis can be either "dual," in which case we maintain the sense of ourselves apart from the object of our concentration, or "merged," when we no longer perceive the object to be distinct from ourselves. Of course, when yogis sit in samadhi this intense concentration continues uninterruptedly for hours at a time.

Classical yoga says that the individual soul, once it has reached the pinnacle of the lower samadhis, must develop the ability to discriminate between itself, as pure consciousness, and any material or mental object with which it identifies (e.g., its body, personality, thoughts, etc.). When consciousness drops all support and takes flight into its own formless, absolute nature, we experience asamprajñata samadhi, the state of knowing which transcends knowledge itself. The great third-century Egyptian philosopher Plotinus aptly described this condition as "the flight of the alone to the Alone." As the last verse of the *Yoga Sutra* states, when one attains this state and becomes "established in the higher self" one is fully "liberated," that is, free from all mental and emotional disturbances and the chains of karma. Patanjali considers this non-dual state of absolute consciousness to be the highest goal attainable by humanity.

Now here comes the surprise. The tantric texts explain that all of us experience this highest non-dual state constantly throughout the day. In the *Tripura Rahasya* the wise king Janaka says, "Brief flashes of non-dual consciousness are experienced by everyone, even while they're busy working, but they don't realize it because they don't know what samadhi is. Every waking moment in which one is not engaged in thought or reverie is an example of samadhi. Samadhi merely means the absence of thought." The king points out that if a man doesn't know what an emerald is, he won't recognize one even if it's placed in the palm of his hand. Just so, we fail to recognize and value the fleeting glimpses of non-dual awareness we commonly experience.

In case you're skeptical, consider these examples, offered by Janaka himself, of instants in which the mind simply stops and reveals the bare consciousness behind it.

- Moments of extreme danger. During an accident many people experience that, rather than panicking, a part of their personality seems to split off, and they become a "witness" calmly watching the event.

- The moment after hearing extremely bad news, such as the death of a loved one, which stuns the mind into silence.

- Moments of extreme pleasure (Janaka mentions orgasm) in which we're swept into an exalted state of peace and satisfaction.

- The brief pause between thoughts.

In each of these instants, there is no content or clutter in the mind, and one simply is.

Those of you working with yogic breathing exercises will have noted that during states like these an involuntary suspension of the breath occurs. Advanced yogis and yoginis take advantage of the physiological connection between holding the breath and intensely focused states of awareness. By retaining the breath for long periods of time they can force their brain to stop generating chatter, allowing the light of the higher self to shine unimpeded into physical consciousness. (Don't try this at home. If a person hasn't done extensive preliminary training, prolonged breath retention can cause brain damage.)

According to the ancient texts, if one can grasp and expand these infinitesimal moments of complete tranquility, one can experience the fullest peace and joy imaginable. But here's another surprise: in order to fully appreciate higher states of consciousness, one must return to lower states of consciousness. No one can ever actually "know" they're in a non-dual state, because in that timeless moment there's no one there to realize that he or she is having the experience! Subject and object have both completely melted away—only the "One" (Plotinus' sublime "Alone") remains. The scriptures mention that infants spend much of their time in unmodified states of consciousness, which may be why they often strike us as so blissful and serene, but that certainly doesn't make them liberated beings. One must not merely have the experience of pure awareness, one must also know one is having it. One must return to a dualistic frame of reference, that is, one must remember oneself and start to think again, before one can discriminate, "Hey, that was non-dual awareness! That was samadhi!" Then, Janaka adds, with the help of this type of careful discernment, as well as through unwavering commitment to pursuing the spiritual goal and, finally, through divine grace, one learns to remain in the highest unitary state.

What's in It for Me?

In the yoga tradition, samadhi is used for purposes ranging from the pragmatic to the sublime. It is the portal to the next step of evolution beyond ordinary human awareness, the path leading from the limitations of our five senses to supernormal experiences. The third section of the *Yoga Sutra* details some of the many vistas that open for the yogini who masters the powerfully concentrated states of samadhi. For example, it reports that by focusing on the subconscious impressions in their own mind (or in other people's minds!) with yogic intensity, adepts can peer into their (or our!) past lives. Patanjali even claims that by focusing with samadhi-like intensity on how physical objects are perceived, yoginis gain the ability to become invisible!

Many supernatural powers are mentioned in the *Yoga Sutra*, including precognition, telepathy, clairvoyance, astral travel, and the ability to mentally manipulate matter. Penetrating concentration on the nature of time and space opens the past, present, and future to the yogi's mental gaze and dissolves the constraints of distance. One morning a few years ago I missed my meditation practice; it was one of those days when one crisis followed another literally from the moment I stumbled out of bed, and I didn't have a chance to sit till early afternoon. Just as I closed my eyes to begin meditating, the telephone rang. Ordinarily, serious yoga students aren't supposed to rise from their meditation seat until they've completed their practice unless it's an emergency. (In India, some yogis won't get up even if there is an emergency!) But an inner voice told me "Answer the phone!" so I jumped up to do so.

When I picked up the receiver all I heard was laughter at the other end of the line. My first reaction was, "Oh no, I got up from my practice for a crank call!" Then I recognized the voice—it was one of my meditation teachers from India. "Panditji!" I cried.

"So, I got you up from your meditation!" the pandit teased, laughing at my consternation. I got the point: no more missing my morning meditation, no matter what the excuse.

As many of us who've spent time in the company of meditation masters have experienced for ourselves, the past, present, and future seem to be an open book for these sages. They appear to know everything about us, as if our thoughts, our memories, and our aspirations are a newspaper they can read at their leisure. This is not necessarily a comfortable feeling; in fact it reminds me of Adam and Eve noticing that they were naked when God came walking in the garden. If there's one thing that's impressed me more than any other about the yogis and yoginis of India, it's the humor and compassion with which they deal with us despite their awareness of all the garbage in our minds.

Patanjali makes an important point in his *Yoga Sutra*:

using samadhi as a tool to develop superhuman powers can be a trap. In Sutra 3:37 he flatly calls dabbling in psychic powers an impediment to spiritual development. Such powers simply generate more states of mind, he explains, while the goal of yoga is to move beyond identifying with ever-more-mental states into asamprajñata samadhi, the state of pure being beyond the limited cognitions of the mind.

When Swami Rama first came to the West he was continually playing with reality, reshaping it as if it were a malleable substance. He would make flowers bloom out of season and make gallons of tea flow from a two-pint thermos. Once when someone cussed him out he playfully filled their home with a horrendous stench which remained in the house till the person apologized.

However, it soon became evident that many students were flocking to him not so much out of a sincere desire to undertake yogic disciplines but more out of curiosity to witness the displays of psychic power for which he was famous. At that point he stopped the phenomena almost completely. Later when he returned permanently to India he started to play again, for example challenging doctors to diagnose a medical condition he claimed to be suffering from. The doctors ran tests and X-rays and CT scans and discovered that Swamiji had liver cancer. A few weeks later when he returned for further testing the tumors in his liver were gone—but new growths showed up in his lungs. The next set of scans a few weeks after that showed the lungs were clear—but he now had cancer of the stomach. He was making a point: for adepts who can control their internal mental states, mastery over physical and biological matter is a child's game.

For the rest of us, cancerous tumors are no joke. We can

scarcely imagine a state of mastery where one can order reality around, making tumors come and go at will. Swami Rama spent decades in the Himalayas exploring advanced inner states in order to reach this extraordinary level of yogic competence. Most of us are willing to spend years preparing for a career or working toward a financial goal, but few of us share the commitment to internal life the yogis and yoginis of India display. That's why when a tumor shows up in our body, we're in serious trouble.

Yoga masters rarely train students in advanced yogic states until they have spent years of testing and training. The reason is, obviously, that yogic skills can be used to exploit others or can lead to ego inflation at just the point where the yogi is nearing ego transcendence. I remember Swami Rama once, in a rueful moment of candor, complaining that although we beginning yoga students think the early part of the spiritual path is the hardest and that it gets easier as we move further along, just the opposite is true. "The further you go, the harder it becomes," he admitted. "The temptations are worse." Having an experienced guru around who earlier has walked the same way herself, who is there to perform ego surgery should such an operation become necessary, is always an advantage for sincere students, beginning or advanced.

Samadhi is a tool which can open us to the realms of extrasensory powers or can carry us all the way through to the liberated state. Patanjali advises yoga students not to waste time with psychic powers but to go for the gold: liberation in this very birth. Swami Rama was always emphatic about this, rolling his eyes with disgust when students would whine that it would take them many lifetimes to achieve liberation. "You can do it, you will do it, do it now!" he would shout.

The Enlightened State

A common image of an enlightened being is some unscrubbed yogi sitting stoically in a cave. This probably stems from Patanjali's description of the consciousness of the realized yogi as being completely divorced from the world, for he has developed total dispassion for the activities of life and disgust for his own body. Patanjali reports that this is the highest good. Still, if we're completely honest with ourselves, we're likely to feel there's something wrong with this picture. Sitting in a thoughtless state, full of contempt for physical reality, doesn't sound appealing to us. Perhaps because many of us haven't suffered that much, we're not motivated to undertake the extreme asceticism necessary to achieve a state that puts an end to suffering. Or perhaps, because of our Western values, this much-vaunted state of non-duality sounds unproductive—and it certainly doesn't seem like much fun.

Fortunately the tantric texts admit that we're not out of line in expressing our reservations about this supposed highest state. There's a wonderful story in the *Tripura Rahasya* telling how an enlightened princess, named Hemalekha, from the country of Videha, teaches her husband meditation, gradually leading him to asamprajñata samadhi, non-dual awareness. Once the prince tastes this tranquil, luminous state, he exclaims, "At last I've found total happiness! Nothing I've experienced before in my life compares to this! Please go away and leave me here alone in the peace of my own blissful self. I feel sorry for you, Hemalekha, because even though you know about this state, you're still running around, active in the world, instead of sitting alone quietly, enjoying the tranquility within."

Hemalekha smiles and answers, "Darling, I'm afraid you

haven't learned anything yet. The most supreme state of all is as far from you as the stars. You only experience this great beatitude while you're seated in meditation. What a useless state of consciousness this is, if it disappears when you open your eyes and stand up! Do you think the millions of worlds in the universe will disappear just because you close your eyes in samadhi? You need to see the self not only within but without; you need to recognize that the blissful self within you is the same blissful self shining in all things."

What Hemalekha is talking about is *sahaja* samadhi, the condition in which one is fully cognizant of the highest reality while still functioning in the world. Here one is not merely experiencing unitary consciousness, one is also carrying the force of this realization into daily life. Classical yoga speaks of the isolation of the individual soul from any contact with matter, but the broader system of tantra (of which the eight-limbed yoga of Patanjali forms just a portion) speaks of bringing this supreme state of awareness back into the world, of enlightenment in the world rather than liberation from the world.

Western students often consider the *Yoga Sutra* to be the final authority on yoga. I was shocked when Swami Rama described it as a primer, a beginner's manual. Real yoga—that is, life in union with the One—does not even begin until one can effortlessly maintain the state of samadhi. Spiritual history is filled with striking examples of fully illumined men and women who lived in perpetual samadhi while actively teaching and working in the world, from the Vedic sages in vast antiquity and their illumined wives up through the present day.

One of the most spectacular modern examples is Ammachi, perhaps the best-known saint in India today. She grew up dirt-poor in southwestern India in the 1950s, but never let poverty or the enormous workload her mother left to her distract her from her spiritual quest. If she realized she'd walked several steps without remembering God, she'd run back and take those steps over again, repeating the names of God. By her teen years she was often found sitting along the seashore near her home, lost in samadhi. She soon became famous for her extraordinary compassion for the poor and oppressed, whom she would move heaven and earth to help.

Penniless as a child, and still living the life of an ascetic today, Ammachi is now head of one of the most massive charitable institutions in India. Each year her devotees build five thousand homes, which they give to poor families free of charge. With volunteer help only, she has built a super specialty hospital in Kerala, which serves the needs of South India's poorest residents without charging a fee. She has also founded schools, ashrams, vocational training institutes, homes for battered women, hospices, and cultural centers, as well as managing a huge South Indian orphanage.

Ammachi personally meets thousands of people—one on one—nearly every day. The lines of people waiting to speak to her at her public appearances in India are literally miles long. She sits all day and night listening to the problems brought to her by rich and poor alike, offering advice, comfort, and affection. What I've found so amazing about Ammachi as I've watched her hour after hour, day after day, attending to the needs of everyone who comes for her help, is that she never leaves the present moment. Ammachi is always fully present with each individual who approaches her, whether it is the first person she meets that day or the five thousandth. She is always relaxed; love radiates from her ceaselessly. She is a breathtaking, living example of sahaja samadhi, of a woman permanently established in the transcendent state who is nonetheless able to work tirelessly at a very practical level here in the material world.

Can we Western students of yoga ever attain such states? We can begin by learning to pay attention to our internal states; we must be alert as we do our practice. As children, we found learning to walk awkward at first; but by paying attention to how it felt in those brief moments when we were perfectly balanced, we gradually learned to stay balanced easily all the time. Just so, we can catch ourselves in those flashing moments of timeless awareness, when our mental tapes are briefly set on "pause," and our real nature has a chance to shine forth uninterruptedly. Then gradually we learn to maintain that state for longer periods of time. In this way we can get to know our real self at last, as the sages of all cultures have from time immemorial. This real self, this unitary, unsleeping state at the root of our being, is our immortal self. The scriptures state that those who constantly abide in this state have attained immortality, because when the physical body falls away at death the mind identifies with the eternal reality within, not with that part of one's being which is perishable. The body gets recycled, its elements returning to the earth, dust to dust. But the inner self continues shining, full of bliss and knowledge. All cultures have beliefs about life after death, because exceptional individuals in virtually every community have had glimpses of this undying inner reality.

At the end of the story about Hemalekha, the prince is now fully enlightened and returns to his castle to resume his responsibilities. His ministers are so impressed by the profound peace and joy he emanates, and with how compassionately and effectively he now behaves, that they ask him to teach them his secret, and they become enlightened too. The common people are astonished by the

change in their ministers (imagine a kingdom full of enlightened bureaucrats!) and demand to know what happened. They start following Hemalekha's teachings also,
and eventually all the people in the country of Videha end
up enlightened! What happens then? No, the whole popula-
tion doesn't retreat to the mountains and caves to sit
around in deep samadhi. Instead, life goes on: merchants
still buy and sell, farmers still work the soil, couples still
love each other, and parents still cherish their children.
But instead of spending their time gossiping about each
other and undermining each other's efforts, the people of
Videha joyfully discuss the wonderful revelations they are
experiencing. Artists now produce works of the highest cali-
ber, reflecting their beautiful new inner visions. Teachers,
instead of rehashing information they have learned from
books, reveal the wisdom they have discovered within
themselves. And the people all lovingly respect each other
as manifestations of the Divine Being itself.

The yoga scriptures make the point that we too can
transform our society into Videha, which means "land of
wisdom," by opening ourselves to the immortal, blissful
luminosity revealed in samadhi, which radiates perennially
in our hearts.

chapter five

Is There Meditation After Death?

A WOMAN IN her mid-40s, the story goes, was killed in an accident. As she floated up out of her body she saw a blazing white light approaching her, radiating perfect, unconditional love.

"Who are you?" the light asked.

"I am Mrs. Alan Jones. My husband is a doctor," she replied.

"I didn't ask who your husband was. I asked who you are," the light said.

"I'm a mother. I have three children: Jason, Joan, and Alyson."

"I didn't ask who your children were. I asked who you are."

"I'm an elementary school teacher. I teach grades three and four."

"I didn't ask what work you did. I asked who you are."

"I'm a Christian. I believe in Jesus Christ."

"I didn't ask what religion you belonged to. I asked who you are."

With a shock, the woman realized she didn't actually know who she was. "I can't answer that," she finally admitted.

With infinite compassion the blazing white light sent her back to Earth, into a new body, in order to find out.

So here we are, just like Mrs. Alan Jones, still trying to figure out who we are. And until we find out, we'll keep coming back, according to the yoga tradition.

"You are not the body. You are not the breath. You are not the senses or the mind," Swami Rama repeated again and again. "You are an immortal traveler. You are *atman*, the infinite."

The Gnostics (Christians and Jews from the first few centuries A.D.) as well as the Sufis said something very similar. They taught that we are princes and princesses from a land of light, sent here on an important mission. There is something extraordinarily valuable—a pearl of great price—we must retrieve for our father, the king. But, wrapped in the cumbersome cloak of a body, we became cold and thirsty and stopped in a tavern to rest. One drink followed another, and here we sit in a drunken stupor, our original mission completely forgotten.

In the yoga tradition the pearl of great price we were sent to find is called the *bindu*, the point of light yogis focus on in deep meditation. It represents knowledge of the self, the living experience that our innermost soul is a being of light, an immortal traveler whose essence is infinite consciousness.

Modern astrophysics and ancient yogic cosmology agree that this entire universe was once contained in a bindu, an infinitesimally small point of infinitely great energy. Atoms are bindus, too, tiny points of matter from which enormous amounts of energy can be released. Our higher self is also a bindu, "smaller than the smallest, vaster than the most vast," according to the yoga texts. When we penetrate the bindu of our higher self, vast amounts of energy are released. The resultant explosion is called cosmic consciousness. Atman, the immortal traveler within, merges with Brahman, the infinite, all-pervading divine being.

We have to jump through a few hoops before we get to that level, though. For the Gnostics and Sufis, as well as for the yogi, our day-to-day experience here in this world is both an adventure and a test. It's a tough exam that takes some of us lifetimes to pass.

The Kobayashi Maru

Star Trek fans are aware that students at Star Fleet Academy (where Star Trek officers like James T. Kirk and Captain Picard were trained) fear nothing more than the Kobayashi Maru, one of the final tests administered before graduation. In the history of the Academy only one student has ever passed that exam. The second Star Trek movie, *The Wrath of Khan*, opens with a Vulcan student named Saavik apparently sailing through the test. In a realistic simulation of space flight, she is very capably captaining a starship—but then suddenly a crisis arises. Saavik receives a distress call from a disabled fuel carrier, but going to its rescue means entering the Neutral Zone, a buffer region between the United Federation of Planets (of which Earth is a member) and the evil Klingon Empire. If she fails to respond, three hundred passengers on the carrier will die. If she moves to save them, she may provoke a war with the Klingons.

Helping space-farers in distress is a Star Fleet officer's first priority, so Saavik cautiously navigates her starship into the Neutral Zone. Instantly Klingon warships materialize and blast her ship to pieces.

Saavik, a logically minded Vulcan, is deeply disturbed by her failure, particularly since she doesn't understand what she could possibly have done to pass the test. There doesn't appear to be any realistic solution to the problem. At the end of the movie James Kirk admits to her that the Kobayashi Maru is deliberately configured so that no matter how the student responds, her ship will be destroyed. The exam has no "correct answer." It is not a test of knowledge or skill, it is a test of character. It is designed to reveal how students react under stress, whether they are more strongly motivated by compassion for others or concern for their own ship's safety.

Like Saavik, all of us are failing the Kobayashi Maru. We are continually confronted with ethical dilemmas to which there is not necessarily any "correct" way to respond; no matter what we do, someone gets hurt. No one wins, and in the end we all die anyway, and everything we've ever worked for blows away in the wind. But passing the test still seems important to us: ending poverty, ending war, ending injustice and oppression. Perhaps to the intelligences who created this *lila*, or divine game, whether we succeed is not as important as that we try. It's a test of character.

But Saavik, along with every other Star Fleet student, knows that Admiral James T. Kirk passed the Kobayashi Maru when he was a cadet—they just don't know how. But if he did it, she tells him, surely so can they. Kirk answers that he was so traumatized at having lost his ship and crew in the simulation that he begged his professors to let him take the test again. Knowing he would fail no matter how many times he tried, they agreed. That night Kirk snuck into the Star Fleet Academy computer center and reprogrammed the simulation. The next day, to everyone's astonishment, he navigated his starship back home, the disabled fuel carrier in tow—and immediately admitted how he'd beaten the program. His delighted professors gave him highest marks for his refusal to give up, for his dogged determination to bring his crew members (even though they were only simulated) safely home.

Spiritual masters are those fortunate few who know how to get themselves and their disciples out of the long-playing game of birth and death; they know how to reprogram the time/space simulation where the rest of us are still taking the test. According to the *Yoga Sutra* advanced yogis can manipulate the elements of matter and energy much as the rest of us manipulate the images in a daydream. Most of us cycle from the waking state, to the dream state, to deep sleep, and back. Yogis establish their awareness in a fourth state, a lucid witnessing consciousness from which life and death seem to be passing dreams. Meditation is the door through which one steps into this superconscious state.

"Beam Me Up, Scotty"

Ammachi tells the story of the little boy who was ill and convinced that the only way he could be cured was by taking a medicine made from a particular herb which grew only at the bottom of a deep pit. The boy kept badgering his father to help him, until finally his dad lowered him down into the pit at the end of a long, strong rope.

At first the boy wasn't afraid, because he knew his father was holding the other end of the rope. But as the pit got deeper and darker and damper the boy became disoriented. The bottom of the pit was thick with mud, very difficult to stand on. He kept slipping and stumbling, getting dirtier and dirtier, more tired, more disgusted, and more frightened.

Clutching the healing herb he had finally found, the boy

started to cry. His father heard him and immediately tugged on the rope, pulling his son back out of the dark hole. This is why we need to cry to God, Ammachi says. When our prayers are heartfelt, the response is instantaneous. Nothing can prevent God's grace from hoisting us back into the light—nothing other than we ourselves untying the rope that connects us, breaking the connection with our divine spirit. We have to remember who we are—children of spirit from a land of light—and keep the connection strong through prayer, meditation, and an intimate, loving relationship with our higher self. Mantra is the long, strong rope dangling down into our ordinary awareness by which our superconscious self pulls us up out of the pit of birth and death. But how does mantra meditation work?

The Sound of Silence

I had been one of Swami Rama's students for over a year without having asked for a personal mantra. The $40 initiation fee was waived for the poor, but I was embarrassed to admit how desperately broke I was. (Swami Rama didn't charge for mantras when he first arrived in the West—it was against his principles to turn spirituality into a business. However, he soon learned that some Americans thought the mantras he was giving weren't any good. The logic behind this was that Maharishi Mahesh Yogi was charging $75 for his mantras, while Swamiji's were obviously far less valuable since they were free. In complete disgust Swami Rama started charging a fee.) Swamiji eventually guessed what was going on, and sent his secretary over to invite me to the Glenview ashram that very night: he would initiate me himself, for free.

It turned out to be the worst possible time. Swamiji was already late for a plane; Kevin was parked outside the ashram entrance with the engine running, anxious to begin the race to O'Hare Airport. When Swamiji approached I blurted out, "We don't have to do this now. Let's do it at some time that's more convenient for you." As relaxed as if he had all the time in the world, Swamiji invited me into his tiny office behind the reception area.

First Swamiji asked me a few questions about my practice. Then he reviewed the basic elements of meditation: a relaxed, upright posture; slow, smooth, even, diaphragmatic breathing; systematic relaxation. And then he gave me my mantra. He spoke it not only with his mouth—the sound seemed to resonate from his entire body! It was really extraordinary. The mantra was the most beautiful, most cosmic sound I'd ever heard. Swamiji asked me to repeat it several times to make sure I was pronouncing it correctly. Then he wrote it down on a sheet of paper, along with a list of nine blessings that emanate from it.

Finally Swamiji indicated the chakra I was supposed to focus on during meditation, and as he pointed toward my heart I felt a rush of energy in my chest that caught me completely off guard. It was as if the mantra were being tangibly transferred into my body. He asked me to repeat the mantra with full attention during meditation and to remember it as much as possible during the rest of the day.

I felt a horrible pang of guilt when I saw Kevin the next morning, fearing that Swamiji must have missed his plane because he'd stayed late to initiate me. "Oh, no problem," Kevin assured me. "It turned out that the flight was delayed for two hours. They had just started boarding when we pulled up."

Over the course of my studies with him, Swami Rama took pains to explain the significance of mantra practice. The mantra is a sound from the soul of the universe, he said. But what he meant by sound was radically different from what most of us here in the West mean by the word. In the yoga tradition sound is understood to be a far more complex and multidimensional phenomenon. The sounds we hear with our ears are only the first and perhaps least important of the four levels of sound energy that yogis work with.

Beyond physical noise comes a second level of vibrations that generally no one but you can hear: the sound of your own thoughts. When you think, you can distinctly hear words in your brain. While physical sounds travel through the air, according to the yogis the sound of thought travels through the akasha, the material of which "empty" space is made. You can hear these sounds if your inner ear is appropriately attuned. This sometimes works spontaneously in emergencies. You may be taking your clothes out of the dryer when suddenly inside your mind you hear your brother calling, "Help me! I fell!" He could be several miles away, but you hear his call as distinctly as if he's in the next room. This is called clairaudience and is one of the skills some yogis cultivate.

The third level of sound is pure meaning itself. You're standing by the dryer when you suddenly get a powerful, sickening sense that your brother is in trouble. You don't hear any inner words, but you know something's wrong. It's possible to hear with the external ear, with the inner ear, and even, as in this case, directly with the mind itself. This is called mental telepathy; many advanced meditators experience telepathy to greater or lesser degrees.

The fourth level of sound, paradoxically, is silence. But just as space is an actual substance, so silence in a sense is actually sound. You experience total silence in deep sleep, yet when you awake your thoughts and personality are still here. They weren't erased by the silence, they were inherent in it, ready to spill out once again when you returned to conscious awareness. Just so, silence is pregnant with meaning; the baby hasn't been born yet, but is definitely gestating in the *hiranyagarbha*, the "luminous womb" of stillness.

Mantras emanate from this living silence, which is permeated with fields of intelligent energy that yogis call *devatas*. Very advanced masters cognize the mantras in silence and bring them down to the mental level, then down to the level of the inner senses, and finally down to the physical level of sound as most of us know it. When your guru initiates you, he or she speaks the mantra into your ear. You repeat it over and over again, syllable by syllable, your inner voice speaking the mantra to your inner ear. Eventually the mantra begins to repeat itself, flashing in the field of your awareness not as a distinct sound but as an intuitive feeling, a force-field of divine intelligence pulsing in your mind. And then the mantra leads your attention into the living silence of your own innermost being.

The Anchor Point

The mantra is our anchor point during meditation. You may have noticed that if someone has a TV on in a room you're in, even if you have no interest in the program your eyes automatically track to the images flickering across the screen. Just so, before our mind is well under control, while we're trying to focus on the mantra our attention is continually being wrenched back to our emotions, memories, and the planning department in our mind. We remember something that happened, we make mental arrangements for something we need to do, we daydream, and we react viscerally to the images that attract or repel us during our reverie.

Fighting with the mind during meditation is useless.

The mind is always going to be thinking; that's its nature. Even during deep sleep *manas*, the subtle matter which comprises our conscious mind, continues ruminating, just as a pot of soup continues to boil whether we're there watching it or not. However, we are not the mind, Swami Rama often repeated. He urged us to constantly remind ourselves, "I have a mind, but I am not the mind." This means that we can let the mind do its thing, but we don't need to pay attention. Our consciousness itself, the will with which we direct our awareness, and the discriminating power which allows us to decide where we wish to turn our attention, lie outside the mind. During the process of *pratyahara* described by Patanjali in the *Yoga Sutra* we withdraw our attention from our body, from our breath, and then from our thoughts and feelings, finally centering it in pure awareness itself.

When they reach the state of pure awareness, beginning meditators find out in a hurry what *vasanas* are. These are the subtle energies playing beneath the surface of our day-to-day awareness; they arise from our *chitta*, our mental storehouse. The subconscious motivating factors stored here determine much of what we do during the day, driving our unconscious actions and reactions. In meditation they come screaming for our attention. We may be able to follow our mantra into inner silence and find the experience of pure self-awareness refreshing and exhilarating, but a split second after reaching that level of composure a vasana impinges on our consciousness: "Gosh, that person I met at the mall sure was attractive . . . I absolutely hate my sister-in-law. How could any human being be so despicable? . . . If I complete my next project ahead of schedule my supervisor may recommend me for a promotion . . . Several houses in this neighborhood have been burglarized in the past two weeks. What if the burglar breaks in here? . . . I'm so constipated . . ." It's amazing how clearly we see our unconscious preoccupations in meditation.

Getting caught up in our vasanas is like fertilizing a weed: this helps its roots grow deeper. So we need to observe our vasanas dispassionately, like we'd watch cross-traffic passing by at an intersection, and return to our mantra. Steering our attention away from the contents of the mind back to the mantra keeps our meditation on course. The mantra's protective field safeguards us from our subconscious, which is calling for our attention, whether it's saying, "Help, I'm frightened," "Wow, this is cool," "Aren't I supposed to be seeing a blue light?" or "I am Xanton of the planet Axia. I have chosen you to channel my message to humanity." Don't be fooled by your vasanas. Return to your mantra. Vasanas melt in the heat of focused yogic concentration. Thoughts fall away. Eventually the mind becomes still.

If you should have any frightening or confusing experience in meditation, speak with your meditation teacher. The vast majority of meditators do just fine, but a few occasionally mistake subconscious impulses for guidance from the superconscious. If you're not sure which is which, sit down with a qualified teacher who's familiar with the tricks the subconscious plays, and let him or her advise you.

At this point it is critically important for yoga students to distinguish between sattvic stillness and tamasic stillness. In a sattvic state, you feel relaxed but fully alert, vividly conscious. In a tamasic state, you feel unfocused. Your mind is comparatively quiet, but you have no sense of your higher self shining within you. People who use drugs to propel themselves into altered states of consciousness may feel a pleasant sense of torpor, but it is difficult to grow spiritually if you are mired in this state. Sattvic stillness leads you to inner illumination. Tamasic stillness leads you to lassitude and sleep.

Many Westerners have no inner life to speak of, other than the occasional lurid fantasy. Their senses are directed entirely outward. They fill every moment of their lives with one form of distraction or another; even watching a vacuous TV show is preferable to sitting alone with themselves. For these people every experience in life has had shape and color and sound and surface. In deep meditation we enter a realm beyond form; there is nothing familiar here to those whose whole life has been centered outside themselves, and so occasionally beginning meditators react to their inner states with fear. They're like landlubbers going to sea for the first time: the deck feels like it's dropping away as the boat rolls, and the new sailor feels a bit disoriented. In the living presence of one's higher self the sense of time and space seem to fall away; there's no gravity for the mind. It's like a space walk in the limitless inner sky of consciousness. In reality there is nothing to be afraid of. It's just a question of reorienting oneself to the universe turned inside out: what was hidden inside the recesses of your soul suddenly surrounds you on every side. It's a wonderful, vivid experience, timeless and pure. The word "adamantine" is sometimes applied to this state because even though it involves letting go of every tangible thing, it feels absolutely solid.

If you should feel unsettled during your meditation, return at once to your anchor point, the mantra. Its protective energy both grounds and elevates the mind, grounding it with audible sound, elevating it beyond the senses to calm inner alertness. Please don't underestimate the power of mantra—especially a mantra originally bestowed by a realized master and passed down through the ages by a vibrant spiritual lineage, repeated billions of times by many thousands of meditators. The guru shakti—the current of enlightenment—flows through it.

Centers of Consciousness

When you are initiated, your teacher may instruct you to hold your focus at some point in your body during meditation, most commonly at your heart or the center between the eyebrows. These are two of the famous seven chakras, so much discussed and so little understood by Westerners. The chakras are centers of consciousness associated with large nerve plexuses or important glands in the physical body; each represents a nexus of a particular type of awareness. Whether or not you accept the literal existence of the chakras, you'll notice that as you move your attention up and down your torso and inside your brain that there are certain points where your consciousness abruptly becomes very clear and expansive, as if a flywheel suddenly locked into gear. These focal points are the chakras. You will quickly note that there are more than seven.

About three inches deep into the brain behind the meeting point of the eyebrows lies the well-known *ajña* chakra, or third eye. Close above it lies the less well-known soma chakra, from which drips the nectar of inner delight. Western scientists conceptualize this as pleasure-giving endorphins being released in the brain, producing the "peak experience" familiar to athletes, artists, and meditators. Above the soma chakra lies the *jñana* chakra, where the fire of discriminating wisdom blazes. Yogis offer their vasanas and all other obstructions to their spiritual practice into this sacred fire, intently visualizing their bad habits and negative thoughts burning to ashes. According to the *Yoga Sutra*, when the seeds of our vasanas are "roasted" in the fire of discriminating wisdom, they lose the power to germinate. Negative tendencies vanish; the light of penetrating intelligence instead shines forth.

Other important chakras include those in the hands, which can be used to transmit healing energy, or those in the feet. In India realized souls are believed to be so spiritually energized that by touching the chakra in their feet the disciple receives a current of blessing energy. Still other chakras, such as the *hara* center emphasized in the martial arts, are activated for purposes such as enhancing one's vital force. An illumined teacher can help you identify the chakra it would be most helpful for you to work with. It then becomes a resonant chamber from which your mantra is continually sounding, and this sets up a current of blessing and protection that surrounds you like a force-field.

I strongly advise that if you'd like to work with the chakras, you seek advice from experienced teachers initiated in an authentic tradition who've developed their awareness through years of spiritual practice. Sometimes New Age teachers, with great enthusiasm but not always much practical knowledge, set up shop and offer classes purporting to teach you about your chakras. But this is an immensely profound and complex science; someone who has not done years of intensive meditation is not likely to have mastered the subject in any depth.

Hidden Light

Recently my neighbor's daughter noticed the sun for the first time in her young life. "What's that ball?" she demanded, pointing to the sky. She may never have seen the sun before, but without its light she wouldn't be able to see anything at all.

For some people, it's not until they begin to meditate that they become aware of their higher self. Yet without this inner sun we wouldn't be aware of our own thoughts, our senses couldn't operate, and the vital force that gives life to our body would never function. Many—perhaps most—people go through their entire lives without becoming aware of the source of consciousness within, the font of life and light.

According to Swami Rama, meditating is a dress rehearsal for death. At death the breath stops, the senses fail, the mind slows and flickers out. What is left? The higher self, the immortal traveler who changes bodies the way we change clothes at the end of the day. Most of us are terrified of death because the only self we know is our body and mind. The yogis, however, have practiced dying, withdrawing the searchlight of their focused attention from the body, slowing the breath, transcending their thoughts, pulling their awareness back to its source, resting their attention in the inner self, the one who never dies. Swamiji explained that yogis don't fear death, "because they know where they're going." They've been that way many times before. Remaining in a state of meditation—that is, remaining continually aware of their inner light throughout life and beyond—the realized masters are never afraid. "Enlightenment," Swamiji specified, "means freedom from fear."

We don't need to turn on our inner light. Like the sun, it's always shining. We just need to look up and be aware that it's there. This is what meditation is for.

According to Shankaracharya, one of the greatest sages of Swami Rama's ancient tradition, there is only one inner light. We have five fingers, but they're all attached to the same hand. There may be billions of people on Earth, but the same inner light shines in us all. "The sage sees the self in all beings, and all beings in the self," says the *Isha Upanishad*. "What sorrow, what delusion can there be for him who beholds that oneness?"

The *Brihadaranyaka Upanishad* explains, "As a web is emitted by a spider which then walks along it, as many tiny sparks fly from one great fire, even so from the one self came forth all worlds, all forces of nature, and all living beings."

For most of us the goals of life are having fun, making money, and living a good, honest life. The *sanatana dharma*, the eternal religion of India, acknowledges these as worthy goals, but adds one more: getting to know the self. "Whoever leaves this world without knowing the imperishable inner self experiences misery and fear after death," the *Brihadaranyaka Upanishad* continues. "But whoever leaves this world knowing the immortal inner self is established in the supreme reality."

After death the realized masters experience freedom from the wheel of rebirth. For the rest of us, yet another physical incarnation rolls around. What can we do about it?

chapter six

Planning Your Next Incarnation

SEEMS LIKE EVERYONE is planning for retirement these days. Everyone's talking about no-load funds, certificates of deposit, IRA accounts, foreign bonds, and those fabulous but volatile technology stocks. The odd thing is, very few people are preparing for what comes after retirement: death, the disembodied state, and reincarnation.

A reader once asked Marilyn Vos Savant (author of the "Ask Marilyn" column in *Parade* magazine) how she coped with the fact that she would die one day. Vos Savant, reputedly one of the most intelligent people in America, answered, "For most of us . . . thoughts of our eventual expiration dates are a big waste of time."

Really? If you or your partner is pregnant, you are certainly making plans to make sure that the birth experience is as easy and pleasant as possible. Shouldn't we make an effort to see that our transition to the next state of being is also painless and positive? If we were moving permanently to another country and couldn't take much with us, wouldn't we plan carefully? Shakespeare calls death "the undiscovered country"; surely this great journey, which we will all take one day, deserves at least as much attention as a trip to Hawaii.

Traditionally, yoga masters in India asked their students to keep the fleeting nature of life constantly in mind and remember that each action we perform here and now will have repercussions in our lives to come.

Our Karmic Credit Line

Today, however, we put our faith in whatever security banks and the stock market can provide. Two thousand years ago a great master from Palestine suggested that we take a different approach: "Don't store up for yourselves treasures on Earth, where moths and rust can consume them and thieves can break in and steal. Instead store treasures for yourselves in heaven, which no moths or rust can destroy and no thieves can take from you." (Matthew 6:19–20)

"You can't take it with you, so enjoy it now" is the advice we get instead. But according to the yoga tradition there is a treasure we definitely do take with us into the next life and beyond: the merit we earn through our selfless actions in this lifetime, by the heightened states of awareness developed in meditation, and by conscious living. At some point we will all lose our bodies, our possessions, and our associates, but our karma will follow us as surely as night follows day. The massive Indian epic called the *Mahabharata* tells us that the results of the deeds we've performed in the past will seek us out in future incarnations as surely as a calf easily finds its mother no matter how large the herd of cows. For this reason it's important to consider on a daily basis what kind of thoughts and actions we're adding to our karmic balance sheet. Yama Raja, the lord of death, cannot be bought off with bank notes or credit cards. The type of experience he assigns us in the next phase of our existence depends on whether there is genuine gold or just junk bonds in our karmic account.

It's not hard to see karmic forces actually at work. As many a parent has noted, newborn infants already exhibit distinct personality traits. Yogis say this reveals qualities the children cultivated in past lives. No child is born a *tabula rasa*, a blank slate on which heredity and environment eventually scrawl their influences. We each come in with a heavy load of baggage called *prarabdha karma*, unconscious conditioning factors which determine our likes and dislikes, our talents and weaknesses, and major events destined to occur in our present life.

For my husband and me, the concept of prarabdha karma is no longer theoretical. I had been studying Vedic astrology, one of the six sacred yoga sciences. Since most of us can't remember our previous lives and therefore have little idea of what our karma in this life may be, the sages of ancient India developed this astrology of the soul, based on our thoughts and behavior in past incarnations, to help us understand what our lessons in this life are. (This is very different from Western astrology, which is personality-oriented.) In Vedic astrology strongly placed planets reveal areas where we worked hard to improve ourselves in past lives; weak planets reveal where we failed. Our yogic horoscope functions much like a spiritual report card.

My husband's birth chart unambiguously shows that he would suffer from a very serious disease, while my own horoscope just as clearly confirms that my husband would undergo a major health crisis. The week Johnathan entered the planetary cycle associated with debilitating illness, he was diagnosed with cancer. My own Vedic chart showed that I'd undergo one of the major traumas of my life that very week. Believe me, learning that my husband—not yet in his mid-forties—might die in the near future was about as traumatic an event as I'd ever experienced! Often the calamities that strike us seem arbitrary and unfair. In this case there was no getting around the fact that this disaster was fore-ordained in our Vedic horoscopes; from the moment of our births we were destined to test our spiritual growth in the crucible of this terrible disease. I could hardly have asked for a clearer example of prarabdha karma playing out in our lives.

Managing Your Karmic Portfolio

I've given a lot of thought to the karmic process over the past few years, particularly as I sat in the oncology ward at Stanford University Hospital where my husband was treated, and watched the horrible suffering and extraordinary heroism of the cancer patients there. It made me wonder how the way I'm responding to this crisis now will affect my experiences in my next incarnation. I've sought advice from various swamis, pandits, and saints, and would like to share some of their insights with you.

The first thing I learned was that in beginning to identify karmic patterns, we have no right to place blame. Just after the Oklahoma City bombing in which 165 people, including many children, were killed, a New Age-inspired acquaintance of mine announced, "You know, those victims were just getting what they deserved. They probably killed someone else in their previous lives." I can't begin to express how shocked I was to hear the law of karma interpreted in such an uncompassionate and superficial manner.

Swami Rama insisted that most karma is actually group karma. In a country like the United States, which has a high tolerance for crime and allows easy access to guns and explosives, innocent victims are continually being swept into the karmic maelstrom of America's pervasive violence. In Norway, where I spent much of my childhood, violence is not tolerated and young men are expected to find constructive uses for their energies other than joining gangs or killing people. In fact, the murder rate in most Norwegian cities is about one or two killings per century. Due to the peace-loving karma of the Scandinavian people, very few fall victim to violent crime in Norway. (It's no coincidence that the Nobel Peace Prize is awarded in Oslo.) We must beware of claiming that the victim of a natural disaster, a crime, or some other calamity is "getting their just deserts." They may in fact be suffering the fruits of the negative behavior of their community or nation as a whole.

Second, it is not necessarily true that bad events arise from bad karma or that good luck and easy circumstances in life mean that an individual has fabulous karma. Almost every teacher I spoke with explained that when we commit ourselves to spiritual life, things will probably get more challenging, not less so. When the Divine Mother wants to accelerate our spiritual growth, it's said she sends one major problem after another, since sorrow so often motivates us to intensify our spiritual practices much more effectively than happiness and tranquility.

Third, it's important to remember that most karma is not written in stone. Many yogic techniques have been developed to help us modify our karma, in effect redesigning our destiny. One of the top astrologers in India advises yoga students to not even bother learning about their horoscopes, because as soon as they start sincerely practicing yoga they begin to rewrite their birth charts. This ability to recreate our future is called *kriyaman karma*, which refers to how the thoughts, words, and actions we're performing right now may be redirecting the course of the karma we set in motion in the past. A horoscope can only reveal our karmic status up to the moment of our birth, obviously. Any activity we currently undertake in full consciousness and with a positive and selfless attitude is helping to alter the flow of our destiny for the better.

Designing Your Next Life

Given the mechanics of the karmic process, what can we do to ensure a tranquil after-death experience and a positive, spiritually focused rebirth?

Chant your mantra. Swami Rama encouraged his students to chant their mantra continually for many reasons. As its divine vibrations reverberate in the subtle body, the subconscious mind is cleansed, and the *devata* (the blessing energy inherent in the mantra) is released. However, Swamiji also emphasized, "At the time of death, mantra is your only friend."

Some people wear gemstones or talismans for luck. These aren't much help after death. But if the mind is saturated with the spiritual vibrations of the mantra, then as the conscious mind fades away at death and the dream-like subconscious rises to dominate the mind-field, instead of fear or regret taking over one's consciousness, the steady protective force of the mantra guides one through the after-death state.

According to the yoga tradition, one's last thought in this life is an extremely potent vector in shaping one's next life. A woman who apparently died in a state of terror while drowning, for example, was documented by a psychiatrist as being extremely phobic about water in this life. In a famous case reported in India, a woman who died in screaming agony during childbirth refused to have relations with men in her present incarnation, she was so afraid of becoming pregnant again.

If through years of mantra practice one has trained one's mind to keep the mantra going continually, even when the mental focus is turned elsewhere and even in sleep, then he or she can be assured that the mantra, one's divine inner friend, will be on hand throughout the death experience to help one remain centered and fearless. If the mantra is one's last thought in this life, its intelligent power helps direct the inner stream of consciousness toward a spiritually focused rebirth.

Define your dharma. If karma is the energy of the past pushing us forward, willingly or unwillingly, dharma is our future goal pulling us forward. Our dharma is what we were born to do, the duty we took birth to fulfill. I have friends who knew from early childhood why they were here—to be a mother, to heal others, to serve their guru. I have other friends, some of them in their forties and fifties, who still have no clue what their dharma is. They feel they are floundering in life, trying to find the reason they're here, looking for some way they can serve others and hopefully support themselves at the same time.

Indian astrologers looking at my birth chart can immediately tell that I'm a writer—my dharma is clearly illustrated there. They can also tell that my husband is attracted to technically oriented, scientific work. But in some horoscopes no clear vocational direction is indicated. As one pandit explained, this is both a liability and an opportunity. Some of us have fairly fixed karma: if a person is born to be an artist, for example, no other options may satisfy her, no matter how much her family may pressure her to pursue some other career. Those born with no clear draw to any particular vocation may feel like they're lost. But on the other hand their future is wide open: by consciously cultivating a specially selected field of interest they can create their own vocation (and thus their dharma) from many choices.

Bill Clinton, the U.S. president, knew from childhood that he wanted to be a leader, and started following his dharma early. In his twenties he was already governor of Arkansas and well on his way along the road to the White House. On the other hand, John Kennedy Jr., in spite of tremendous pressure from family and friends to follow his father's footsteps into politics, spent his twenties searching out what he really wanted to do. Finally in his thirties he combined two strong interests, and helped found a new political magazine. Clearly Clinton had defined and aggressively pursued his political goals in previous lives; in this lifetime he used that momentum to propel himself to leadership of the Free World. Kennedy, however, created his own dharma in his short life.

In South and Central Asia we see many examples of those who define their own dharmic path and very consciously set specific future lives into motion. In both the yogic and Buddhist traditions, spiritual aspirants can determine to spend their future lives serving humanity, teaching spirituality, becoming enlightened themselves, and liberating others. Advanced yogis and lamas envision their future lives with such clarity that they can actually announce when and where they will be reborn. Their intense sense of purpose—the desire to alleviate the suffering of others—gives them such a strong commitment to fulfilling their dharma that the laws of nature bow before them, allowing them to take rebirth precisely as they have predicted.

Examine your motivations. Do we, as yoga students, have the ability to precisely shape our next incarnation, as the yogic adepts and lamas do? To do so, each of us first needs to ask ourselves: are we just going with the flow of our karma, or are we consciously directing that flow to ensure that our future lives will be better and brighter and more serviceful? What is it we're here to accomplish? What are our long-term goals?—i.e., our goals not just for this life but for the lives to come? What sorts of karmic vectors are we setting in motion right now? Are they rooted in selfishness, greed, and pride, or in compassion, clarity, and tranquility?

We need to take seriously the prospect that all the psychic energy we're generating today will definitely come back to us. When we inevitably face the fruits of our karma will we be relieved, or appalled? Are the work, the relationships, and the thought-life we're engaged in now contributing to the person we want to become, not just in this life but in the next, or are we merely creating obstacles for ourselves, problems that sooner or later we'll be forced to deal with?

When we look honestly at how we're living our lives we give ourselves the ability to alter our course for the better, and we begin to work intelligently with the powerful dynamics of karma.

Meditate. In order to reach our inner light, our innate intuitive and healing power, the source from which reliable guidance and unshakable tranquility emanate, we must reach deep into ourselves, and for this meditation is indispensable. It is meditation which puts us in touch with the undying part of our being which fully understands what our purpose in the material world is, how we can achieve our aims here and hereafter, and how we can bring healing, balance, and insight into our lives on earth.

In meditation we move beyond the sensations in our physical body, beyond the physiologically regulating impulses of our prana, beyond the chatter in our mind, into a center of intuitive awareness and serene joy. It's like reaching the top of a mountain: suddenly we have an outstanding view. In the clear atmosphere of our higher self we can see our way, what we're doing right, what we're doing wrong, where we're coming from, where we need to go. When we mentally make ourselves a promise ("I'm going to be more positive about my job," "I'm not going to get mad at my sister-in-law anymore") so often it seems to evaporate into thin air the next moment. But seeds consciously planted in deep states of concentration ("This life is full of joy and loving service," "My next birth will be among loving, spiritual parents, and I myself will be loving and spiritual," spoken not so much with words but with a deep inner sense of assurance) are far more likely to take root and grow, sheltered by the divine grace which permeates these inner states.

Live your affirmations. Be what you want to become. If you hope to be less selfish in your next birth, start practicing now. If you hope that in your next incarnation you won't be as concerned about money, stop worrying about it so much now. Even small efforts to physically incarnate your ideals can have big payoffs as the positive things you affirm about yourself become anchored in physical reality. Remember that things you wish for extremely intensely (whether they're truly good for you or not) may become your actual experiences in another birth even if they're impossible to achieve in this one. Therefore always use your *buddhi*, your discriminating intelligence, to choose wisely the things you want and what you'd like to become. Then accelerate the fruition of the karma you have consciously created by starting to live it in the here and now.

Do unto others. Whatever we do to others will be done to us. The yogis know that if there's something you want, give it away. If you would like to be wealthy in your next birth, be generous in this one. If you would like a beautiful home in the future, help create a warm and welcoming home where you are right now. If you hope that others will help you in your next life, become a helpful person yourself. If you want good parents, friends, and a happy marriage in your next incarnation, be an outstanding parent, friend, and partner in this life. Whatever you pass along to others today—whether it's loving friendship, or financial support, or hatred, or jealousy—will be reflected back to you in your next life. For every action there is an equal and opposite reaction.

In India to this day one occasionally sees ascetics who have given away all their possessions and are practicing severe austerity for the ironic purpose of becoming rich in the next life. They give up the things they desire now in the hope of being amply rewarded in the future. The basic principle is to do unto others as you would have them do unto you, and recognize that sacrifices made on behalf of others will always be repaid, though not necessarily in this life.

Practice self-control. If we make no other efforts to plan our future lives, the least we can do is practice a basic level of sense control. While we assume that we will be reborn as a human being, according to the yoga masters this isn't necessarily true. If a person leads an animal-like existence, preoccupied with food, sex, and dominance, the door to future lives in the animal world remains open. The yoga tradition warns that even advanced masters have fallen back into animal births when they weren't careful. If we want a human body we need to cultivate the human rather than the animal qualities in ourselves. And according to the tradition, if we are continually preoccupied with divine things we may even raise ourselves to a divine state and be reborn in a higher world than this physical realm. But there is also the danger that those who are ridden with craving or despair may be reborn in hellish, ghostlike states.

Accept your karma gracefully. It would be nice to think that by carefully regulating our thoughts and actions we could direct the course of our future lives entirely. However, there are always events and circumstances in our lives that remain out of our control: the vast storehouse of karmic tendencies dogging us from numerous previous incarnations; group karma which may override our personal karma; divine will and the guru's grace, which can reorder reality at their pleasure.

Since our terribly uncomfortable encounter with prarabdha karma three years ago, when my husband's cancer was first diagnosed, he and I have been working hard to clear our karmic accounts, investing a lot more time in spiritual practices, and working to generate good karma to nullify the challenging karma currently enveloping us. But there comes a time when the only viable response to the karmic nexus we're caught in is to surrender to the process itself and trust that the outcome—if we don't resist it—will be to our spiritual benefit. Dealing with cancer has been the most difficult experience of my life, yet also the most spiritually maturing. This world really is a school for souls and our karma is our personally custom-designed teacher. Sometimes the lessons are easy, and other times they're really tough. We can maximize our experience here by taking our spiritual practices seriously, and allowing the grace that flows from those practices to design our next incarnation for us.

"Know thyself." Who precisely is it who reincarnates? Is it the pure, lucid conscious being we sense within ourselves in deep meditation? The yoga tradition answers no, that pure awareness never goes anywhere, it's never born and it never dies. Is it our personality, the thinking being we experience ourselves to be in the present moment? Yoga says no. If it were our ordinary mental state that reincarnated, we would distinctly remember who we were in our last lives; there would be no break in our awareness from birth to birth.

As we progress in meditation we begin to distinctly experience the different "layers" of our being. These are precisely outlined in the yoga tradition.

First, there is the *annamaya kosha*, which literally means "the body made of food," the material body. Second, there is the *pranamaya kosha*, or "body made of vital energy," the organizing field which animates the physical body. If you have difficulty grasping the distinction between these layers, think of a stillborn infant or a corpse. In these two cases you are looking at a material body from which the pranic body is absent. Unless it is permeated by a life-infusing field of prana, the physical body immediately begins to rot; the force of entropy takes over and it disintegrates into dust. Yogis keep their physical body healthy by carefully regulating their diet and practicing hatha postures. They invigorate their pranic body or vital energy by practicing pranayama, breath control. The simple breathing exercises we learn in our yoga classes are our first steps toward learning to control the energy-field that sustains life in our physical body.

The pranic body is the vehicle for life, but it has no inherent life of its own. At the time of death it, like the physical body, dissipates into its component parts, returning to nature.

Yogis call the third layer of our being the *manomaya kosha*, or "the body made of thought." This consists of the thoughts and feelings continually playing across the screen of our awareness. In the West many religious people call this our soul, and believe this part of ourselves will continue to exist forever, either in heaven or hell. According to the yoga tradition, however, this "mental body" is also mortal. It continues to exist for a time after death as the soul reviews its thoughts and actions during its previous life, but this mental self fades away before rebirth, allowing a fresh mental being—a new personality—to begin evolving at the time of rebirth.

Spiritual practices involving mantra repetition or visualization begin at the mental level but are designed to lead us inward to still more subtle layers of our being.

The fourth level of our being is the *vijñanamaya kosha*, or "body made of intuitive knowledge." You begin to experience this level in meditation when you move beyond body awareness, beyond sense perceptions, and beyond thought. Here you experience intuitive insight, radical insight, pure inspiration. How many times have you mentally wrestled with a problem, and only when you finally relaxed and stopped hunting for a solution did the answer occur to you? Yogis would say your attention shifted from the mental body with its limited resources of logic and reasoning into the intuitive body with its vastly expanded capabilities. The mental self relies on the input of your five senses, but the intuitive self is geared toward the all-encompassing knowledge of the higher self, which gives you access to information you couldn't possibly gather from sense data alone. The greatest scientists, artists, and statesmen are able to shift their awareness into the vijñanamaya kosha and find their inspiration there.

One of the most important purposes of meditation is to

help us lift our day-to-day consciousness from preoccupation with our body and thoughts into that part of ourselves permeated with *vijñana*, intuitive insight. When we begin to live and work from this level our lives become filled with creative power, healing ability, charisma, and the transformative force we in the West rather wistfully call "magic."

The fifth and most subtle layer is called the *anandamaya kosha*, or "the body made of bliss." This is the level of pure joy that mystics are familiar with, the "peak experience" of great athletes, the indescribable ecstasy each of us has experienced in the highest moments of our lives. It is an exaltation of spirit beyond words, an immersion in absolute beauty, truth, and beatitude. This is the last shout of worship and adoration before our soul dissolves in the soul of all, the explosion of consciousness that occurs as the inner self steps into the living presence of God. For those of us who've caught glimpses of this depth of our being in intense meditation, it's as if our consciousness shoots out the top of our head like a rocket, and we're left stunned into speechlessness in pure delight at the great *lila*, the perfect divine play, of the Mother of the Universe.

The fourth and fifth levels, the body of intuition and the body of bliss, are the vehicles of consciousness that reincarnate. Yogis achieve a sort of semi-immortality by transferring their focus of awareness from the life of the body and mind into the interior life of the higher reincarnating self. This is how they avoid losing consciousness in the after-death state and how they can take a new birth (or borrow any adult body which might have become available!) in full awareness. Working through the two inner bodies which do not perish during death, they are no longer subject to the wheel of mortality on which the rest of us spin. Realized masters watch their disciples carefully to see who is progressing in meditation and may finally have advanced enough to be initiated into the mysteries of the fourth and fifth bodies. This is a level of development most of us in the West don't even think about, yet this—immortality—is the aim of most yogis and yoginis in the East. No wonder they take the science of meditation so seriously!

At the moment of final liberation, the yogini renounces even these subtlemost portions of her being and dissolves her individual consciousness in universal awareness. As Shankaracharya, one of the greatest masters of the yoga tradition, explained, "atman is Brahman"—that is, our own innermost self is ultimately one with the divine consciousness, just as a wave is ultimately no different from the ocean that is its true being.

In meditation we pay attention to the inner components of our nature. We learn who we really are, we start to live consciously, we become the architects of our destiny rather than the victims of karma, and we begin the journey back to our source. The key, as the sages have always insisted, is to "know thyself." Meditation is the way.

Karmic Divestiture

Many of us in the West think of our sadhana in terms of short-range goals. We want to be healthy and young-looking, so we sign up for hatha classes. We want to avoid the disease and mental agitation caused by stress, so we sit for meditation. Even India's most ancient surviving scriptures, the Vedas, consist largely of hymns asking for a better life: success, wealth, a loving marriage partner, healthy children, freedom from fear. These are legitimate goals in the Hindu tradition, but they are not the goals of the yogi. The ultimate aim of yoga is not creating a better future life by improving one's karma, but freeing oneself from the constraints of karma altogether. *Moksha* and *mukti,* words often translated "enlightenment," literally mean "freedom"—that is, freedom from karma. Yoga science explains that in the highest states of meditation the seeds of karma we carry with us from birth to birth are "roasted" in the fire of divine knowledge and can therefore no longer germinate. When a yogi is established in this state, he or she is free from the bondage of karma and can move about in this world, or any other realm, liberated from karmic compulsions. Liberated beings live spontaneously in the present, blessing everyone around them by their mere presence. Miracles occur in the presence of these great beings because karmic law breaks down in their company. Through the practice of karma yoga—giving up the fruits of all their actions and not expecting any reward for their selflessness—these saints have mastered the karmic process itself. Fully identified with their higher self, which clings to nothing in this world, they become conduits for peace and healing.

It's important to keep the real goal of yoga before us, but until we reach the state of the enlightened masters it may be prudent for us to manage our karma wisely, bearing in mind that our thoughts, words, and actions will have concrete effects for us in the future, in this life or the next. If we plan for our future lives as scrupulously as we plan for a vacation or our retirement, we will have invested wisely indeed.

My experience with the saints and yogis of India is that they take the long-range view. They see our present problems, our strengths, and our spiritual aspirations in the context of numerous previous births. They are incredibly patient with us because they also see our enormous potential—we are enlightened masters in the making. Our higher self, the enlightened master within us, is already present. The guru's job is to help us be what we already are, to bring that enlightened awareness into our day-to-day consciousness. Our job is to take our sadhana seriously, to make an unwavering commitment to spiritual life.

Those of us who have spent time in the company of great yoga masters know how joyful they are, how much they laugh, what fun life is for them. It's a challenge but also a wonderful pleasure to live and work in their presence. Sadhana entails self-discipline, but in the yoga tradition this is less a penance than an adventure. We are on the frontier of vast new realms. What an opportunity!

chapter seven

Living Miraculously

INDIA IS SUCH A TRIP, if you haven't experienced it yourself, you won't be able to imagine it. They have phones there but the phones don't work, they have faxes and e-mail but these don't work either. If you try to turn on a lamp you'll discover that the electricity comes and goes erratically, like lightning during a thunderstorm. Driving through New Delhi one day I spotted a sight I'd never seen before in all of India: a working traffic light. As I turned to point it out to my husband, our taxi driver sped right through it—he had no idea what the red light meant.

My in-laws have been to India several times. Whenever they had a flight scheduled, they would get to the airport an hour and a half early to check in, as we do in the U.S. Twice they arrived at their gate only to discover that their plane had already departed; the pilot didn't feel like waiting around for the passengers. This was not some podunk airline, this was the major Indian airline.

At every leg of our travels through India our reservations got completely mixed up. Fearing the worst, I contacted our travel agent to double-check and then triple-check our tickets for the return trip home from Calcutta to Seattle. But it was not until my husband and I were actually boarding our flight that we discovered the plane was bound for Seoul, Korea. Our travel agent had typed SEO instead of SEA into his computer.

It always amazes me when I hear people say they're going to "do" India. First they'll do Europe, then maybe they'll do Turkey, and then they'll do India. You don't do India—India does you. It's completely useless to make plans there, because Mother India has plans for you that you can't even imagine. The whole time we were in India we never got where we intended to go, but we always got exactly where we were supposed to be. Mother India was making our travel arrangements for us.

Here in the West we live in a culture where the electricity works and the phones work and science works. In India logic breaks down completely, but telepathy works, clairvoyance works, and precognition works. In India, I'm telling you, the laws of physics are different. If you immerse yourself in Indian culture like we did, you will literally experience time and space completely differently. For example, in the United States a day is about six hours long. In India, however, twenty-four hours last about six days. The pace of life is so different there, the part of your brain that's conditioned to rush, rush, rush burns out like an overloaded fuse. Your rational mind shuts down. And suddenly—magic happens.

There's not a lot of magic left in the West. In India magic still reverberates through the forests and villages, the mountains and cities, the rivers and temples. Blink once and a monkey materializes beside you chattering an urgent message from Hanuman, the monkey god. Blink twice and your sputtering rental car carries you all the way from Bengal to Bihar even though you're out of gas. Blink three times and a tourist from western Germany is assuring you there are no spiritual masters left in India. Blink again and you find spiritual masters everywhere.

Some Westerners fight India the whole time they're there; they want the comforts and the structure they're used to, and they have an awful time. But those who surrender to India pass through an invisible portal into a mystical kingdom where yogis and yoginis still range like the soft-hearted sorcerers and white witches of our children's fantasy books, trailing events we call miracles, but they call yoga science.

Here in the West we're convinced that all of human history slowly wound its way from primitive cavemen toward its supreme climax: us and our technology and our science. In India I saw men and women who still live in caves like their ancestors did tens of thousands of years ago, so backward they don't wear clothes, so primitive some of them don't even have fire. They're called yogis, and they are the most advanced human beings on the face of the Earth.

Yogis at Work

Swami Rama rarely spoke about his guru, Bengali Baba. He was extremely careful to avoid offering clues as to where in the Himalayas we might find the adept, protecting his privacy till Bengali Baba vacated his body in 1982. So it was quite a surprise for us to discover just how well-known Swami Rama's guru actually is in India. The legendary adept is considered to be one of the greatest yogis of the twentieth century, and several Indian films have been made about his life.

Bengali Baba was recognized as a master of *parakaya pravesha*, the science of transferring one's consciousness into another body (a technique he demonstrated on several occasions). But he was most famous for his command over the forces of life and death, even in the event of someone else's demise. When the prince of Bhawal died suddenly some decades ago, for example, his family wrapped him in funerary linens and began burning his corpse. Monsoon rains put out the fire and swept the body into the river. Several miles downstream Bengali Baba instructed his disciples to pull the body out of the water and unwrap it. Then he restored the prince to consciousness (interpret this any way you're able to deal with it—I'm just reporting the facts) and taught him the inner essence of the yoga tradition. Eventually the prince returned home, where his family was not happy to see him. His considerable land and fortune had already been divided up between his heirs, none of whom wished to surrender their inheritance. In one of the most famous and thoroughly documented cases in Indian judiciary history, the prince was able to prove he was indeed himself, his recent death notwithstanding, and got his property back. Bengali Baba became one of the best-known masters in South Asia—and fled into the mountains to avoid further publicity.

The stories get even wilder. When one of my teachers, Swami Satyananda Saraswati, travels on pilgrimage through north India, he stays in the cave of the immortal sage Markandeya. The cave extends deep into the mountain. Benches of stone have been cut into the rock to accommodate the yogis living in the cave, where they remain in unbroken meditation for weeks at a time. Some of them claim to have actually seen Markandeya, though they admit he comes and goes very mysteriously.

Markandeya's story begins billions of years ago. According to the yoga tradition, not only are individuals born again, planets and even entire world systems also reincarnate. Markandeya was born during the last incarnation of our solar system—or to be more specific, he was almost not born during the last incarnation of our solar system. His mother was having a difficult time getting pregnant, so she and her husband went to consult their local astrologer.

Checking their stars, the astrologer counseled, "Yes, I see the blockage in your childbearing karma right here in the fifth house of your horoscope. Due to the ill effects of actions you performed in your past lives, you were not destined to have children in this lifetime. Nevertheless, by conscientiously performing the spiritual practices I will assign you, you can partially change the flow of your karma so that you will be able to bear one child. But because your bad karma from the past must still have some effect, the birth of your child will cause you great sorrow. So choose: you may either have a stupid, selfish, materialistic son who will live many long years, or a brilliant, devoted, highly spiritual son who will die before his sixteenth birthday."

The would-be parents were in shock. But quickly they agreed to do the penance the astrologer prescribed if only they could have the wonderful though short-lived son the soothsayer promised.

Nine months later Markandeya came toddling into the world. He was everything his parents had hoped for and more: highly intelligent, selfless, pure-hearted, and a true spiritual prodigy. For years the couple pressed the astrologer's ominous prediction out of their minds, but as the boy's sixteenth birthday approached, they became increasingly distraught.

Markandeya noticed that his parents were unhappy, but neither would tell him the cause. Finally, the day before his fateful birthday, Markandeya found his mother collapsed on the floor, prostrate with grief. Enough was enough: the boy ran to his father and demanded to know what was going on. No longer able to conceal his tears, his father explained about the bargain they'd made with the astrologer, and told Markandeya he had only a few more hours to live.

Markandeya was horrified. As a sincere spiritual aspirant he had meditated regularly, hoping some day to achieve enlightenment. But he hadn't realized he had so little time. And now he was about to die without having achieved any of his goals! The boy ran sobbing to the local Shiva temple, and threw his arms around the image of the Supreme Being, Lord Shiva, at the altar.

Then, as Markandeya sat weeping and clinging to Shiva, Yama Raja entered the temple. Yama is the lord of death, the incorruptible instrument of karma sent to collect each of us at our appointed time.

"Shiva, please help me!" Markandeya cried out with innocent faith, and as Yama began to slip his noose over the boy's neck, Lord Shiva himself materialized before them. "You dare disturb my devotee while his mind is fixed on me?" Shiva demanded, raising his trident as if to kill death. Yama Raja fled in terror, and since Markandeya's pure mind never leaves the feet of the Supreme Lord, Yama has been afraid to carry Markandeya to the land of the dead all these billions of years. Even after the sun exploded and the atoms of our previous solar system scattered into space, Markandeya did not die. Floating in space, he watched while a small eternity passed till our solar system once more began to coalesce, and Earth reformed into the globe we live on now.

Obviously—to our Western minds—this is a fable somebody made up. But here's the funny thing: Markandeya's report about how solar systems come into being and end, recorded in ancient Sanskrit texts called *Puranas*, were confirmed by Western astrophysicists in the twentieth century. As recently as the nineteenth century, Western scholars scoffed at the description of our sun ending its days as an exploding red star and at the multi-billion-year age of Earth given in these texts. Most of them still believed Earth was a mere six thousand years old. Other bits of information purportedly passed to the yogis by Markandeya included the true shape of Earth (a bulging ball) and the fact that the sun rather than Earth lies at the center of our local world system. All this was virtually unknown to the Western world till comparatively recently. I remember Carl Sagan, the late and slightly bombastic science educator, commenting on the striking parallels between ancient Indian teachings and modern cosmology. It's an "astonishing coincidence!" he declared. That's the thing about the yoga tradition: the more you learn about it, the more astonishing coincidences you uncover.

Maybe a yogi billions of years old really does live in the Himalayas, maybe not. But someone needs to explain how ancient "primitive cavemen" of the Himalayas acquired astronomical information thousands of years in advance of their time. We may well also inquire what other knowledge the yoga tradition has preserved that remains centuries ahead of what we in the West know today. If yogis like Bengali Baba can transfer their awareness into other bodies, not to mention "raising" people the rest of us understand to be dead, Western scientists have a long way to go to catch up.

Breakfast with Yama Raja

Yama Raja has been playing a large role in my life these last few years, as have the Himalayan masters. I'd been terrified of death since early childhood, and years of meditation hadn't slaked my fear. I had prayed to the Divine Mother to help me overcome my feelings—and unfortunately she responded.

My husband is an exceptionally mature person spiritually; when he was diagnosed with Ewing's sarcoma (a very serious form of bone cancer for which the odds of surviving are poor), he accepted the reality with composure. I, however, was hysterical. Friends thought I was dealing with the crisis well, but inwardly I was falling apart. Suddenly Yama Raja, the lord of death, was sitting down with us for breakfast every morning. There is nowhere to escape when he looks you in the eye. You can't run to the future, fantasizing that everything is going to be just fine. You can't run to the past, remembering how wonderful your life was before this happened. Instead you're frozen in the present moment, with Yama Raja's icy breath flowing down your neck.

We look around and the material world seems so solid. Our bodies seem so real. Then suddenly death walks in the room and you realize that in the next moment the walls and the furniture and the floor may fade away as your body stops functioning. Your plans and aspirations, your deeply felt political views, your exciting career goals, your stock portfolio, everything that just a moment ago seemed so vitally important now winks away as if you'd changed the channel on your television screen. Our life here is the briefest visit; we fell in through the mysterious portal of birth and now we're about to fall out through the gaping gate of death. How dreamlike life suddenly seems! I finally understood the Sanskrit word *maya*: it doesn't mean this world isn't real; it means this world is evanescent—it passes in and out of existence like a rain cloud on a stormy day.

But to think of Yama Raja as a malevolent force is to

mistake his nature. In the West we call Adam the first man ever to walk our Earth. In much of the East, Yama is known as the first human being. He appeared on our planet, they say, during the Golden Age when peace and justice pervaded the world, and he was a just and compassionate man. As the first man to be born, however, he was also the first to die. And as the first human consciousness to enter the after-death state, he claimed that realm as his own, becoming the king of death, Yama Raja. But because he was just and compassionate, he also made an extraordinary promise. "I will remain here in this place, guiding every soul who passes through death safely into my realm," he vowed. "Showing partiality toward none, I will assign to each soul the rewards or punishments they deserve based on their thoughts and actions during life. And when their stay in my kingdom is complete I will show them the way back to the world of matter, where they can finish their spiritual journey."

Some of those who have undergone near-death experiences have reported encounters with Yama Raja, experiencing him as an infinitely wise and loving entity who eased their fear, had them review their lives here on Earth, and helped them to understand the consequences of both their selfish and unselfish actions.

Sadly, most of us approach death like blind people groping in darkness, consoling each other with platitudes like, "Oh, she's in heaven with the angels now," because we don't really have a clue about what happens after death or even if there is a life after death. Swami Rama explained that yogis don't fear death because "they know where they're going." Having explored the inner worlds during deep levels of meditation, they have long since made peace with Yama Raja. They know his world and many worlds beyond.

My friend Cathy was approaching fifty. She'd had many romances but had never been married. Finally she decided to approach Ammachi, the great saint of south India, to ask for her blessing in finding a husband. Ammachi's response to her request shocked Cathy to her bones. "Many women spend hours in front of the mirror putting on makeup and adjusting their hair," she said. "Who spends even a few minutes preparing for death?"

Cathy immediately grasped what Ammachi was saying: that she wasn't a teenager anymore and that she was approaching a time in her life when spiritual practice, not romance, should be her central preoccupation. Ammachi was not predicting that Cathy was about to die, but she was saying, in essence, "Get your priorities straight."

Everything about contemporary Western culture is geared toward seducing us away from our inner spirit. Our central concerns become how we look, how much money we make, buying a sports utility van or a cappucino maker. Our relationship with a potential lover, our supervisor, our pet, are far more vital to us than our relationship with our own soul. Meditation is the only boat sailing against this current. Instead of leading to more grasping, meditation shows us how to detach our inner self from constant craving. Instead of directing us outward through our five senses, it redirects us toward the inner organ of intuition, a way of knowing that doesn't depend on seeing or hearing or touch. It reorients us from space and time to consciousness and eternity.

The Play of the Goddess

In India, time, the force that ultimately annihilates the entire universe, is called the goddess Kali. She comes in different forms. For example, you may have experienced a crisis in which you turned within and called out for help from the depth of your heart, and by the time you finished your prayer the problem was resolved—some remarkable breakthrough removed your difficulty. Hindus might say that the Divine Mother came to you in the form of Durga, the goddess of victory, who appears instantly to save her devotee.

At other times she comes as Kali, the goddess with the bloody fangs and the hacked limbs hanging from her belt. Kali comes not to change the awful circumstances you find yourself in; Kali comes to change you. She doesn't put out the fire, she makes you walk through it. Kali is the fire.

My husband is very close to one of the greatest saints of north India, Shree Maa of Kamakhya, a devotee of the goddess Kali. The day after we received the devastating news of how critically ill Johnathan actually was, we got a phone call from our local Hindu temple. Shree Maa had just canceled the rest of her tour through north India and caught a plane to the United States. She was on her way to our house.

Shree Maa sat with Johnathan for hours, singing to the Mother Kali and running her hands through his hair. She is the purest human being I've ever seen, utterly transparent to divine peace. Born to one of the wealthiest families in India, as a teenager she ran away from her opulent home in Assam to wander through the Himalayas, where mountain people would find her sitting in samadhi for days on end, completely absorbed in the divine world. Sitting with Johnathan in our meditation room, her perfect tranquility suffused my soul. I finally realized that, whatever the outcome, this awful experience was wholly in the hands of the Mother of the Universe.

The next morning we received a call from Johnathan's

oncologist. He was deeply apologetic—there had been a mistake in Johnathan's diagnosis. All the previous test results pointed to Ewing's sarcoma, but the final test showed that in fact Johnathan had a different form of cancer, one that was much easier to treat. I would later learn, after having spoken with all the oncologists in the department, that none of them in their entire professional careers had ever seen a case where a tumor that clearly presented as a sarcoma turned out to be this far-less-deadly form of cancer. But then they'd never seen Dr. Shree Maa at work before, either.

There are different ways to look at an experience like this. The way I see it is that Shree Maa slightly adjusted our karma. It was our destiny to go through this struggle with cancer—Shree Maa did not remove the disease. But she altered the situation just a bit so that we were able to go through the experience a little more easily and yet still learn a great deal from it!

Not long afterward we had another lesson in how grace can do an end run around the laws of causality to help us when we're in serious trouble. This experience involved our friend Bhagavan Das. If you've been around the Eastern spirituality circuit as long as I have, you'll remember a book that came out in the early 1970s by Ram Dass called *Be Here Now*. In it Ram Dass tells how while traveling through India he met a tall blond spiritual seeker from Laguna Beach, California, named Bhagavan Das. Every time Ram Dass would ruminate about things that had happened to him, Bhagavan Das would counsel, "Don't think about the past. Just be here now." Each time Ram Dass would worry about what was going to happen the next day, Bhagavan Das would counsel, "Don't worry about the future. Just be here now." It was Bhagavan Das who first introduced Ram Dass to his guru, Neem Karoli

Baba. Bhagavan Das is one of my husband's great spiritual heroes.

Even though Johnathan did not have Ewing's sarcoma, he still had to go through chemotherapy. Considering all he'd been through, he underwent his treatment with extraordinary grace and humor. But I will always remember the night he got so sick from the chemo he was ready to die. Johnathan does not give up easily, and seeing him in a state of such total despair shook me profoundly. My knees gave way and I sank to the bedroom floor. "Divine Mother," I prayed, "Johnathan needs your help right now. I know you usually make us wait for an answer to our prayers, but he needs help this very instant."

That moment, the doorbell rang. It was Bhagavan Das. He swept into our home, immediately grasped what was happening with my husband, swept Johnathan up in his arms, and started singing bhajans to the Divine Mother in his typical, open-hearted way, snapping Johnathan right out of his depression.

Later I asked, "Bhagavan Das, we haven't seen you in months. How did you happen to come to our door at that exact moment?"

Bhagavan Das said he hadn't planned to stop by our house. He was on his way from Lake County down to San Francisco; in fact he was already well past our exit on the highway. Then as he was driving through Marin County he suddenly heard a voice say, "Turn the car around. Go see Johnathan. Now." Bhagavan Das swung his van around and raced all the way to Sonoma.

Afterwards I calculated that it would have taken him at least thirty minutes to get from Marin to our home in Sonoma. He must have heard the voice a good half hour before I even said my prayer. Then I remembered how Pandit Tigunait used to tell me that shakti, divine power, is not limited by time or space. If we cry out from the depths of our soul to the Divine Being, it can literally rearrange the course of history in order to come to our aid.

Often it takes a serious crisis to put us in touch with the miraculous powers that underpin the universe. In the *Bhagavad Gita* Lord Krishna says that four kinds of people seek the divine: those who are suffering terribly are often the first to cry out to a higher power; those obsessed with obtaining some material goal, who realize they can't achieve that goal by their own efforts alone, also resort to prayer; those who desire spiritual knowledge ("What is the nature of this universe? How am I to understand God—or myself?") turn to the divine within in their quest for truth; but the greatest of the seekers, says Krishna, is the one who turns to a higher being out of sheer love.

Many of us yoga students may ask how we can love a nameless, faceless, formless reality that is utterly beyond the ability of our mind to comprehend? It's one thing to love a wife or boyfriend or your child—someone you can wrap your arms around, who answers you in plain English when you speak to them. It's another to love a spiritual being you can't touch or see, and whose answers to your prayers are by no means always clear.

Living Divinity

Years ago I was on my way to see the great Indian saint Ammachi. Many of us who have spent time in her presence agree that she is the embodiment of unconditional love, as if she were the Divine Mother herself in human form. As one Hindu newspaper put it, she is "a supernova of spirituality," revealing by her moment-to-moment example what tireless selfless service actually entails.

The temple where Ammachi was scheduled to appear

that evening was reeking of incense. Nothing triggers migraines for me faster than strong smells, and within minutes I was reeling with a brain-splitting headache. I knew I would have to leave—if I stayed any longer I would be vomiting with pain by the time Ammachi arrived.

As I walked through the woods back to the hut where I'd left my backpack, I started to sob uncontrollably. I had come so far to be in the presence of this great soul, yet just before seeing her I had been forced to leave. The experience seemed so bitterly symbolic of my entire life: yearning to enter the living presence of the divine, yet because of my inherent unworthiness, my lack of capacity, I was a constant spiritual failure.

I stepped into the hut to collect my things—and did a double take. Incredibly, there was Ammachi sitting in the room, smiling up at me. "Daughter, daughter, why are you crying?" she called. "Mother is always with you!"

Here I thought I wouldn't see Ammachi, and the whole time she was sitting waiting for me!

When we become discouraged about our spiritual practice, when it seems as if we try and try but don't get anywhere, it's imperative to remember that our own inner being, the higher self within us, is waiting and watching and guiding, closer to us than our own thoughts. The divine being is not far away, it's right here, right now—it's always with us. We just have to take down the umbrellas of our doubt and let the ever-flowing grace of the supreme consciousness pour down on us, soaking us through and through.

This great inner being we can't see or hear embraces us more tightly than our own body; it is more fully present than our own unfocused mind. But because we can't see this great one with our five senses, we must learn to meditate so that we can sense its vast, loving presence with our awakened heart.

According to the yoga tradition, the supreme being has two faces: *nirguna* and *saguna*. *Nirguna* means "without qualities." It is that aspect of reality that is utterly beyond the capacity of our mind to grasp, that can only be experienced in deepest meditation: pure awareness itself, which never changes, which is never born and never dies. *Saguna* means "with qualities"—and the foremost divine quality mentioned again and again in yoga's sacred scriptures is unconditional love. "I love you more than you can imagine," says the Divine Mother in the *Tripura Rahasya*. In the *Bhagavad Gita* the Supreme Lord vows, "Meditate on me always, devote all your actions to me, worship me with your whole heart, and I promise you will reach me. This is the truth: I love you exceedingly."

For most of us it may be helpful to conceive of the supreme being as *saguna Brahman*, as a personal divinity such as a divine father or the mother of the universe, rather than as an abstract principle, remembering that we recognize the divine being by one quality: its absolute, limitless love. "No experience in this world gives us unbroken happiness," Ammachi says, "except the love of God, which is limitless." The saints understand that meditation is not a mechanical technique but a living encounter with boundless wisdom, creative power, and unconditional love.

How do we know we are progressing in meditation? "When you are cheerful," Pandit Tigunait told me. Cheerfulness is a sign that the subtlemost layers of the mind are being purified and are becoming transparent to divine love. What should we do when our progress in meditation seems blocked? "Open your heart," Swami Rama told me. "Learn to love all and exclude none." I remember Ammachi gazing affectionately into my typically somber Norwegian face. "Smile," she said.

The last three years, during which we've been struggling with my husband's illness, have been a period of learning to let go of our attachments, to enjoy every day that—through grace—Johnathan and I share together, and to trust in a higher power which somehow seems to be directing our lives. This time has thrown us back intensely on our spiritual practice, which, together with the blessings of our spiritual teachers, has been the source of our strength during very difficult circumstances.

The yogis say that humans occupy a unique place in the cosmos. Unlike the animals and unlike the angels, we have free will. We can choose to honor or reject the divine essence within us, our higher self. Never before in world history has it been more important to make the right choice. When I was a child, we would have a mass murder in the United States every five or six years. Today mass murders happen nearly every week. As I write these words even India, the last stronghold of unbridled mystical experience, is under threat of possible nuclear attack. Everywhere it seems the forces of light are in desperate jeopardy.

When we begin to meditate, we begin to live miraculously. Portals in the inner worlds open and suddenly just the right book, just the right class, just the right teacher comes into our life. Circumstances rearrange themselves to offer us the opportunity to learn exactly the lesson we most urgently need to learn. And just when our faith begins to wane—poof!—magic happens, gentle reminders that we're not alone, that we are being guided. For thousands of years the masters of the yoga lineages have kept the flame of enlightened awareness burning. For thousands of years they have scanned the masses for sincere students to transmit their living experience to. Sincere students like us.

It's not an accident that you're drawn to spiritual life. It's not a coincidence that you have set out on the path of meditation. A great force is drawing you inward. With open hearts and stilled minds may we all pass through the portal. With loving reverence, I bow to the divinity in you.

chapter eight

The Way In: Meditation 101

YOGA STUDENTS KNOW the drill: the importance of sitting in a comfortable, upright position, watching their breath, chanting their mantra. But many still practice meditation as if it were a penance, spiritual drudgery, or a mental chore. They haven't grasped that meditation is actually a divine invocation in which the greatest living spiritual master in the world is invited to come and sit with them.

The great master is one's own higher self. Its living presence is the source of divine knowledge, healing, and creative power.

Saints like Mira Bai, Lalleshvari, and Ramakrishna were actually in love with their inner being, whether they called it Krishna, Shiva, or Kali. In the Christian tradition it is called the Holy Spirit. It is the guru shakti, the living energy of enlightenment.

Sitting in the presence of this majestic being is life-transforming. The body becomes still, the mind becomes tranquil, and one becomes intensely lucid, vividly alive. It's as if the body and mind are in a state of deep sleep except that one's conscious being is absolutely awake. Compared to the living reality of this serene luminosity, our everyday life is a passing dream.

There are no sights or sounds in this state, because one has left the world of names and forms. In this state is pure awareness filled only with itself. Time and space, life and death exist within this radiant beingness, but it is not disturbed by them.

This great living master is none other than our own immortal spirit. To live in its light is what Jesus called "everlasting life."

The Mechanics of Meditation

The rudiments of meditation are so simple it's astonishing that they have such a powerful effect. These simple exercises are the foundation of inner life.

Start your meditation program by determining the amount of time you would like to spend in meditation. For first-timers, ten or fifteen minutes are plenty. Householders who are serious about cultivating a spiritual life ought to spend a minimum of half an hour twice a day in meditation. Yogis and yoginis who have renounced worldly life often spend eight hours a day or more sitting in meditation. Swami Rama once spent eleven months in nearly continuous meditation, shut away in a tiny Himalayan cave.

Sit. Sit up as straight as you can comfortably without straining yourself. This position allows your nervous system (especially your brain and spine) to function optimally and makes a huge difference in the clarity of your awareness.

It may help to imagine a string attached to the top of

your head pulling you into an upright posture. Be sure you're comfortable, because you're going to be sitting in this position for some time. If you catch yourself slumping during your meditation, gently shift back into an upright position. You will probably find that if your attention starts to wander, you unconsciously begin to slump.

Relax. You should hold only enough tension in your body to keep your head and trunk upright. Every other muscle in your body should be relaxed. Mentally scan your facial muscles, arms, hands, torso, abdomen, legs, and feet, checking for tension. Allow any tension you discover to dissolve out of your body like butter melting in the sun.

Breathe. Bring your full attention to your breath. Breathe slowly and smoothly, without any jerks or pauses in the stream of air. Breathe silently: you should barely be able to hear yourself breathe. Don't force yourself to breathe more deeply than feels natural, but allow your breath to find its own comfortable depth.

Now bring your full awareness to the fleshy bridge between your nostrils. Note whether your left or your right nostril is flowing more fully. Feel the coolness of the air as it flows into your nostrils; feel how warm it is as it flows back out.

Never underestimate the power of breath awareness. Because of the intimate link between the respiratory system and the nervous system, directing your breathing into a calm, uninterrupted flow will reciprocally propel your brain into a serene, centered state. Yogis focus on the sensation of air passing in and out of their nostrils until both nostrils flow equally. When this occurs, one enters a state Swami Rama called "joyous mind." In this intensely tranquil, lucid state, meditation is optimized.

Focus. Call your mantra into your awareness. If you don't have a mantra, you may use the universal mantra so-hum. Mentally hear the syllable *so* (as in "Is that so?") as you inhale. Mentally hear the syllable *hum* (as in "I like to hum that tune") as you exhale. In Sanskrit the phrase *so-hum* means "I am he—the higher self." (Some yogis and yoginis chant *sah-hum*, meaning, "I am she—the higher self." The *ah* in *sah* is pronounced as in "Ah, that feels wonderful!")

Beginners mentally repeat their mantras; intermediate meditators hear the mantra repeating itself in the inner sky of their awareness. Advanced meditators no longer hear their mantra at all: the living intelligence of the mantra is flashing spontaneously in the field of their consciousness.

Stay with the mantra. New meditators are often amazed at how difficult this seemingly innocuous instruction is to follow. Distracting thoughts arise continually, like unwelcome visitors pounding on the door. In a fraction of a second we can lose our focus and slip into a state of reverie. Incredibly trivial concerns such as "the floor needs to be washed" may arise with compelling urgency.

Be a witness. Watch the thoughts come and go but don't fuel them by getting emotionally or mentally caught up in them. Instead keep returning to the focus of your attention, to your mantra. Don't fight intruding thoughts, don't judge the images that appear before your mental eye. Just let them go.

There may be things you usually brood about—how someone you particularly dislike treated you, what a friend said, what's happening at work. Resolve that for the duration of your meditation you will not play your usual mental tapes but will stay with the mantra.

If spectacular lights or angel-like beings or verbal instructions from some source apparently outside yourself appear in your awareness, rest assured that they are being projected by your subconscious mind. When students would complain to Swami Rama, "I don't see divine lights in meditation," he would shout, "Good!" Meditation is not about sifting through the debris in your subconscious, no matter how sublime it may seem; it is about propelling yourself into a formless, superconscious state beyond visions and sounds.

Release. At the beginning of your meditation you focused your awareness on the muscles in your body, then you shifted it inward to your breath. Next you moved your awareness to your mental state. Since it is the nature of the mind to continually race from one thought to the next, you stabilized your mental awareness using the tool of your mantra. Like a horse that can't run very far because it's tied to a post, your mental processes are kept in check with the aid of the mantra. You are learning to discipline your mind and consciously direct the flow of your awareness inward, the first step toward attaining samadhi.

Now shift your awareness from your mental state to the inner consciousness from which your thoughts emanate. Your mantra fades into silence, the highest state of mantric awareness. This is an intensely lucid state, analogous to an unflickering, intensely bright light. You are fully awake and alert but are not focused on any object; you are simply abiding in your own nature as consciousness itself. This is an immensely refreshing, spiritually rejuvenating state.

The waking state is consciousness with many objects of awareness. The dream state is unconsciousness with many objects. The deep sleep state is unconsciousness with no objects. Meditation is consciousness with one object, the mantra. The superconscious state is consciousness without any object. Release your awareness into this state and effortlessly remain in that condition for as long as you're able to hold the space.

This concludes your meditation. Return to your workaday awareness, but avoid getting up instantly. If you have the time, spend a few more moments sitting quietly, allowing the serenity you experienced in the superconscious state to suffuse your mind and all the cells of your body.

The Heart of Meditation

The way in is the way out. Suffering and death are inevitable for embodied beings who dwell in space and time, but have no power over the transcendental self, which abides beyond the grasp of space, time, and causation. Our human consciousness gives us the unique ability to turn our awareness from its usual outward flow through our five senses, redirecting it inward to levels of existence our senses cannot perceive. This gives us the potential to consciously make the transition from mortality to immortality. This is the central message of the yoga tradition.

Asato ma sad gamaya.
Tamaso ma jyotir gamaya.
Myrityor ma amritam gamaya.

Lead me from delusion to truth.
Lead me from darkness to light.
Lead me from death to immortality.

What does it mean to be immortal? It certainly doesn't mean to stay in the same physical body forever; some yogis use one body for centuries, but eventually it's less effort to trade it in for a new model than to keep repairing the old one. According to the yogis, immortal sages of antiquity like Dattatreya, Shankaracharya, and Parashurama are still teaching in the Himalayas, whether in the physical body *du jour* or in a disembodied state. Their stream of consciousness is not interrupted by the process of rebirth, during which most of us forget our previous incarnations. No time is wasted relearning forgotten skills.

Near-Eastern-based religions such as Christianity and Islam, which borrowed much of their doctrines from ancient Zoroastrianism, state that following Judgment Day this material world will be immortalized and the dead bodies of believers will be resurrected to live forever in physical form. Orthodox adherents of these faiths also believe the universe was created about 6,000 years ago. The yoga tradition emphatically rejects this view. According to yoga, our Earth is billions of years old and will continue to exist for billions of years more, but ultimately it will dissolve in the searing heat of the dying sun and its atoms will blow away in the cosmic wind. There is no physical immortality, only cycles of becoming, universes breathing themselves into existence and finally expiring. Only spirit lasts forever. By shifting our awareness from the part of ourselves that passes away to the part of ourselves that exists outside time, we can participate in the nature of divinity itself.

The immortal sage Shankaracharya admitted that it's impossible to explain what divinity is since no words can possibly encompass the limitlessness of its being, but three terms come closest to reflecting its nature: *sat, chit,* and *ananda,* pure existence, pure consciousness, and absolute bliss. Ammachi, one of the greatest sages alive today, would add *prema*, unconditional love, to that list. She points out that the universal consciousness has brought us all into being, cares for us, and is training us just like a loving mother.

When we add love to our spiritual practice, reflecting divine love back to the Divine, returning love to its source, we close the circuit of spiritual evolution. Our spiritual practice leaps to life as the enlightening power of guru shakti begins to flow.

That luminous presence we meet in deepest meditation is our beloved self, the self of all beings. "The sage sees all beings in the self, and the self in all beings," say the yoga scriptures. "Therefore he hates no one."

"Love all and exclude none," a Himalayan master I was privileged to study with used to say. It's the same thing as loving your self.

"Love is the most ancient traveler."
—*Swami Rama of the Himalayas*

Glossary of Sanskrit Terms

Ajña chakra. The center of awareness behind the eyebrows; the "third eye."

Akasha. The space from which matter originally emanates.

Ananda. Inner bliss; absolute bliss.

Anandamaya kosha. The body of bliss.

Annamaya kosha. The physical body.

Arati. A ceremony in which a lighted candle is waved in a circle before a picture or statue.

Artha. The good things in life.

Asamprajñata samadhi. The state of pure being beyond the limited cognitions of the mind; non-dual awareness.

Asanas. Hatha yoga postures.

Ashtanga yoga. The "eight limbs" of yoga.

Atman. Pure conscious being within ourselves.

Avatars. Actual incarnations of God.

Bhajans. Devotional songs.

Bhakti. Devotion.

Bindu. A dot or seed. The pinpoint of light on which yogis focus in meditation.

Bodhi chitta. Loving kindness.

Brahman. The supreme reality, absolute consciousness itself.

Buddhi. Discriminating intelligence.

Buddhi sattva. The subtlemost portion of the mind; the purest part of everyday consciousness.

Chakras. Focal points in the subtle body.

Chit. Pure consciousness.

Chitta. Our mental storehouse.

Devata. The blessing energy inherent in the mantra.

Dharma. What we were born to do; the duty we took birth to fulfill.

Dhyana. Meditation.

Durga. Hindu goddess of victory, usually shown riding a lion, carrying weapons of war.

Gayatri mantra. A mantra designed to invoke the light.

Guru. The flow of illuminating power which is the basis of spiritual life; a spiritual teacher.

Guru shakti. The current of enlightenment that flows through the mantra; the living energy of enlightenment.

Hiranyagarbha. The "luminous womb" of stillness.

Ida. The left nerve current in the subtle body.

Ishta devata. Personal deity.

Jñana chakra. The center of discriminating wisdom.

Kali. Hindu goddess of destruction. Despite her terrifying appearance, she is understood to be a loving, motherly deity.

Kama. Sensuality.

Karma. Our thoughts, words, and deeds, and their consequences.

Karma yoga. Selfless service; surrendering the fruits of one's actions.

Kirtan. Singing beautiful devotional songs.

Kriyaman karma. The karma we are generating in the present moment.

Kundalini. The energy of consciousness which moves in the subtle body.

Lila. The random-seeming twists of life, seen as a game the Goddess is playing.

Manas. The thinking portion of our conscious mind.

Manomaya kosha. The mental body.

Mantra. A sound from the soul of the universe; a divine word projected from divine consciousness.

Maya. The insubstantial nature of things, the unreliable, constantly changing face of material reality.

Moksha. Freedom from karma.

Mukti. Freedom from karma.

Nadi shodhanam. Alternate nostril breathing.

Nirguna. Literally, "without qualities," signifying that God's nature is beyond the ability of our minds to understand.

Parakaya pravesha. The technique of transferring one's consciousness into another body.

Parampara. The lineage of gurus extending back to prehistory.

Pingala. The right nerve current in the subtle body.

Prana. The vital force; life energy.

Pranamaya kosha. The field of life energy which animates the physical body.

Pranayama. Yoga breathing exercises.

Prarabdha karma. Unconscious conditioning factors from previous lifetimes which determine our likes and dislikes.

Pratyahara. The process by which we withdraw our attention inward from our body.

Prema. Unconditional love.

Pujas. Rituals in which flowers, incense, grain, etc. are offered to the Divine.

Purusha. The higher self.

Rajas. The principle of activity.

Sadhana. Spiritual practice.

Saguna. Literally, "with qualities," signifying the parts of God's nature we can imagine, such as love, wisdom, etc.

Sahaja samadhi. The condition in which one is fully cognizant of the highest reality while still functioning in the world.

Sahasrara chakra. The center of awareness associated with the uppermost portion of the brain.

Samadhi. The superconscious state; an intensely lucid state in which thought is absent.

Samprajñata samadhi. Superconciousness with an object.

Samyama. The threefold process of concentration, meditation, and samadhi.

Sanatana dharma. The eternal religion of India.

Sandhi. Union; the center between two breaths.

Sat. Pure existence.

Satsanga. Keeping the company of truth; spending time in the presence of one's guru or other saints.

Sattva. The principle of harmony, light; enlightened understanding.

Shabda Brahman. God as waves of primordial energy, experienced in the human brain as sound.

Shakti. The active intelligence of divine being; the energy of illumined awareness.

Shaktipata. The spontaneous transmission of enlightened awareness.

Shiva. Pure consciousness, sometimes symbolized by a naked Hindu deity who is always absorbed in meditation.

So-hum. Literally, "I am that (the higher self)." A mantra synchronized with simple breathing practices.

Soma chakra. The center within the brain from which divine nectar (ecstasy) drips.

Sushumna. The central nerve channel of the subtle body.

Tamas. The principle of inertia.

Tattvas. Subtle elements.

Vak. The primordial divine word; divine intelligence as a creative principle.

Vasanas. The subtle energies playing beneath the surface of our day-to-day awareness. The grooves in which our minds run.

Vidyas. The inner sciences of yoga.

Vijñana. Intuitive insight.

Vijñanamaya kosha. The organ of intuition.

Viveka. Discriminating intelligence.

For Futher Reading

Awaken, Children! Dialogues with Sri Sri Mata Amritanandamayi, Volumes 1-9, Swami Amritasvarupananda. San Ramon, Calif.: Mata Amritanandamayi Center, 1990–1998.

Daughters of the Goddess: The Women Saints of India, Linda Johnsen. St. Paul, Minn.: Yes International Publishers, 1994.

From Death to Birth: Understanding Karma and Reincarnation, Pandit Rajmani Tigunait. Honesdale, Pa.: Himalayan Institute, 1997.

In the Footsteps of the Sages (videotapes), Pandit Rajmani Tigunait. Honesdale, Pa.: Himalayan Institute, 1999.

The Living Goddess: Reclaiming the Tradition of the Mother of the Universe, Linda Johnsen. St. Paul, Minn.: Yes International Publishers, 1999.

Living with the Himalayan Masters, Swami Rama. Honesdale, Pa.: Himalayan Institute, 1999.

Meditation and Its Practice, Swami Rama. Honesdale, Pa.: Himalayan Institute, 1998.

The Nag Hammadi Library, edited by James M. Robinson. New York City: HarperCollins, 1990.

The Power of Mantra and the Mystery of Initiation, Pandit Rajmani Tigunait. Honesdale, Pa.: Himalayan Institute, 1996.

The Puranas, Volumes 1-3, abridged summary by Bibek Debroy and Dipavali Debroy. Delhi, India: B.R. Publishing Corporation, 1994.

The Royal Path: Practical Lessons on Yoga, Swami Rama. Honesdale, Pa.: Himalayan Institute, 1999.

Sakti Sadhana: Steps to Samadhi—A Translation of the Tripura Rahasya, Pandit Rajmani Tigunait. Honesdale, Pa.: Himalayan Institute, 1993.

Shree Maa: The Life of a Saint, Swami Satyananda Sarasvati. Napa, Calif.: Devi Mandir Publications, 1997.

The Song of God: Bhagavad Gita, translated by Swami Prabhavananda and Christopher Isherwood. New York City: New American Library, n.d.

The Upanishads: A New Translation, Volumes 1-4, translated by Swami Nikhilananda. New York City: Ramakrishna-Vivekananda Center, 1977.

Yoga Philosophy of Patanjali [a translation of and commentary on the *Yoga Sutra*], Swami Hariharananda Aranya. Albany, N.Y.: State University of New York Press, 1983.

About the Author

LINDA JOHNSEN is a leading author in the field of Eastern spirituality. Her first book, *Daughters of the Goddess: The Women Saints of India*, was voted "Best New Age Book of the Year" by the Midwest Book Association. Her essays appear in numerous anthologies and she is the author of over 100 magazine articles.

Johnsen earned a master's degree in Eastern Studies and Comparative Psychology at the University of Scranton's innovative program in yoga science and philosophy. She went on to do postgraduate work in Comparative Religion at the Graduate Theological Union in Berkeley. An initiate in the Shakta Advaita tradition of the Great Goddess, she has been active in introducing Jyotish, one of India's yoga systems, to the West.

Johnsen's latest books are *Meditation Is Boring? Putting Life in Your Spiritual Practice* and *The Living Goddess: Reclaiming the Tradition of the Mother of the Universe*. She is currently at work on a book about Western spiritual adepts of the Hellenistic period, focusing on their relationship with the yogis of India. She lives in the San Francisco area with her husband, Johnathan Brown.

The main building of the Institute headquarters, near Honesdale, Pennsylvania.

The Himalayan Institute

FOUNDED IN 1971 by Swami Rama, the Himalayan Institute has been dedicated to helping people grow physically, mentally, and spiritually by combining the best knowledge of both the East and the West.

Our international headquarters is located on a beautiful 400-acre campus in the rolling hills of the Pocono Mountains of northeastern Pennsylvania. The atmosphere here is one to foster growth, increased inner awareness, and calm. Our grounds provide a wonderfully peaceful and healthy setting for our seminars and extended programs. Students from around the world join us here to attend programs in such diverse areas as hatha yoga, meditation, stress reduction, Ayurveda, nutrition, Eastern philosophy, psychology, and other subjects. Whether the programs are for weekend meditation retreats, week-long seminars on spirituality, months-long residential programs, or holistic health services, the attempt here is to provide an environment of gentle inner progress. We invite you to join with us in the ongoing process of personal growth and development.

The Institute is a nonprofit organization. Your membership in the Institute helps to support its programs. Please call or write for information on becoming a member.

Institute Programs, Services, and Facilities

Institute programs share an emphasis on conscious holistic living and personal self-development, including:

Special weekend or extended seminars to teach skills and techniques for increasing your ability to be healthy and enjoy life

Meditation retreats and advanced meditation and philosophical instruction

Vegetarian cooking and nutritional training

Hatha yoga and exercise workshops

Residential programs for self-development

Holistic health services and Ayurvedic Rejuvenation Programs through the Institute's Center for Health and Healing.

A *Quarterly Guide to Programs and Other Offerings* is free within the USA. To request a copy, or for further information, call 800-822-4547 or 570-253-5551, fax 570-253-9078, email bqinfo@himalayaninstitute.org, write the Himalayan Institute, RR 1 Box 400, Honesdale, PA 18431-9706 USA, or visit our website at www. himalayaninstitute.org.

The Himalayan Institute Press

THE HIMALAYAN INSTITUTE PRESS has long been regarded as "The Resource for Holistic Living." We publish dozens of titles, as well as audio and video tapes, that offer practical methods for living harmoniously and achieving inner balance. Our approach addresses the whole person—body, mind, and spirit—integrating the latest scientific knowledge with ancient healing and self-development techniques.

As such, we offer a wide array of titles on physical and psychological health and well-being, spiritual growth through meditation and other yogic practices, as well as translations of yogic scriptures.

Our sidelines include the Japa Kit for meditation practice, the Neti™ Pot, the ideal tool for sinus and allergy sufferers, and The Breath Pillow,™ a unique tool for learning health-supportive diaphragmatic breathing.

Subscriptions are available to a bimonthly magazine, *Yoga International*, which offers thought-provoking articles on all aspects of meditation and yoga, including yoga's sister science, Ayurveda.

For a free catalog call 800-822-4547 or 570-253-5551, email hibooks@himalayaninstitute.org, fax 570-253-6360, write the Himalayan Institute Press, RR 1 Box 405, Honesdale, PA 18431-9709, USA, or visit our website at www.himalayaninstitute.org.